THE JOURNAL OF

CORPORATE CITIZENSHIP

Issue 4
Winter 2001

Theme Issue: **Australasian Perspectives on Corporate Citizenship**

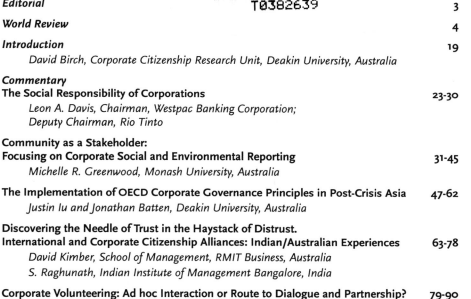

T0382639

© 2001 Greenleaf Publishing Limited.
All written material, unless otherwise stated, is the copyright of
Greenleaf Publishing Limited. Views expressed in articles and letters are
those of the contributors, and not necessarily those of the publisher.

Greenleaf
PUBLISHING

ISSN 1470-5001

THE JOURNAL OF CORPORATE CITIZENSHIP

General Editor   Dr Malcolm McIntosh, Warwick Business School, UK

Publisher   John Stuart, Greenleaf Publishing, UK

Production Editor   Dean Bargh, Greenleaf Publishing, UK

Editorial Assistant   Veronica Towler, New Academy of Business, UK

EDITORIAL BOARD

Professor Carol Adams	University of Glasgow, UK
Dr Jörg Andriof	Visiting Fellow, Warwick Business School, UK
Professor David Birch	Deakin University, Australia
Dr Gill Coleman	New Academy of Business, UK
Dr Jan Jonker	Nijmegen University, Netherlands
Professor Marcelo Paladino	Universidad Austral, Argentina
Maria Sillanpää	KPMG, UK
Professor Sandra Waddock	Boston College, USA
Professor Simon Zadek	Copenhagen Business School, Denmark

REVIEW BOARD

Ian Barney	Swansea University, UK
Dr Simon Collinson	Warwick Business School, UK
Mark Glazebrook	Deakin University, Australia
Dr Brad Googins	Boston College, USA
Adrian Henriques	independent consultant, UK
Rob Lake	Henderson Global Investors, UK
Dr Magnus Macfarlane	Warwick Business School, UK
Dr Craig Mackenzie	Friends Ivory and Sime
Christopher Marsden, OBE	Amnesty International Business Section, UK
Anupama Mohan	Warwick Business School, UK
Dr Eamonn Molloy	Warwick Business School, UK
Dr David Murphy	New Academy of Business, UK
Jane Nelson	Prince of Wales Business Leaders' Forum, UK
Dr Jan Aart Scholte	Centre for Regionalisation and Globalisation, University of Warwick, UK

CORRESPONDENCE

The Journal of Corporate Citizenship encourages response from its readers to any of the issues raised in the journal. All correspondence is welcomed and should be sent to the General Editor at the New Academy of Business, 17–19 Clare Street, Bristol BS1 1XA, UK.

Entries for the 'Diary of Events' and books to be considered for review should be marked for the attention of the Editorial Assistant and sent to Veronica Towler, New Academy of Business, 17–19 Clare Street, Bristol BS1 1XA, UK; veronica.towler@new-academy.ac.uk.

- All articles published in *The Journal of Corporate Citizenship* are assessed by an external panel of business professionals, consultants and academics.

- *The Journal of Corporate Citizenship* is monitored by 'Political Science and Government Abstracts' and 'Sociological Abstracts'.

SUBSCRIPTION RATES

The Journal of Corporate Citizenship is a quarterly journal, appearing in Spring, Summer, Autumn and Winter of each year. Subscription rates for organisations are £150.00 sterling/**US$250.00** for one year (four issues) and for individuals £75.00 sterling/**US$125.00**. Cheques should be made payable to Greenleaf Publishing and sent to:

The Journal of Corporate Citizenship

Greenleaf Publishing Ltd, Aizlewood Business Centre, Aizlewood's Mill, Nursery Street, Sheffield S3 8GG, UK Tel: +44 (0)114 282 3475   Fax: +44 (0)114 282 3476   E-mail: journals@greenleaf-publishing.com. Or order from our website: www.greenleaf-publishing.com.

ADVERTISING

The Journal of Corporate Citizenship will accept a strictly limited amount of display advertising in future issues. It will also be possible to book inserts. Suitable material for promotion includes publications, conferences and consulting services. For details on rates and availability, please e-mail advertising@greenleaf-publishing.com.

Printed on acid-free paper from managed forests by The Cromwell Press, Trowbridge, Wiltshire, UK.

Editorial

Issue 4 *Winter 2001*

Malcolm McIntosh, General Editor
Warwick Business School, UK

IT IS WITH GREAT PLEASURE THAT I introduce this first special edition of *The Journal of Corpororate Citizenship*, compiled by our Guest Editor, Professor David Birch of Deakin University, Australia.

As the discussion of corporate citizenship has developed in recent years, it has been conducted predominantly on the basis of perspectives and voices from North America and Europe. Yet the questions raised by this debate apply as much to business practice and social, enviromental and economical wellbeing in the Southern hemisphere as they do in the Northern, as much outside the English-speaking Judaeo-Christian world as within it.

As I said in the first edition of this journal, one of its roles is to endeavour to develop a greater understanding of corporate citizenship as an international issue—to seek actively to engage some of these other experiences and viewpoints in the ongoing construction of a knowledge-base on this topic, and to honour the work currently being done by scholars in many different countries to explore, understand and communicate the emerging practice of corporate citizenship. This edition, therefore, represents the first of what I hope will be many perspectives from the South, considering the application of new corporate citizenship practices in Asia and Australasia. In particular, it reminds all readers of this journal that openness to 'different' perspectives, and building relationships across cultural and conceptual difference, is a key component of developing better relationships between businesses and the societies within which they sit.

Many thanks to Professor David Birch and colleagues in Melbourne, Australia, for this edition, and may I also extend thanks to our new editorial assistant, Veronica Towler, and to fellow Editorial Board member Dr Gill Coleman at the New Academy of Business in Bristol, England.

World Review

July–September 2001

Jem Bendell

*in association with
the New Academy of Business*

A synopsis of
the key strategic
developments
in corporate
responsibility
around the
globe over the
last quarter

Compact news

THE GLOBAL COMPACT, A UN PROGRAMME intended to help businesses become better corporate citizens, celebrated its first anniversary on 26 July with more than 300 corporate partners, up from 44 at its launch. New UN Assistant Secretary-General Michael Doyle outlined the idea is to use the Global Compact website as the foundation for a learning network where companies can share best practices on CSR. 'It's going to be a genuine learning exchange', he said. Earlier in the month his predecessor, John Ruggie, explained to Warwick University, UK's 4th Annual Corporate Citizenship Conference the plans for the Global Compact Learning Forum, to be based at the university. Professor Ruggie explained that the Compact 'has explicitly adopted a learning approach to inducing corporate change, as opposed to a regulatory approach'. More of his thoughts are summarised in the review of the Warwick conference, on page 14.

After the anniversary, it became clear that some environmental and human rights groups were disappointed that the Global Compact would not be doing more than acting as a learning forum. 'Viewing the program solely as a learning experience represents a wasted opportunity in assuring corporate responsibility,' said Arvind Ganesan, the director of business and human rights programmes for Human Rights Watch. 'The progress we expected on moving beyond just a learning forum hasn't occurred yet.'

While the analysed process of reviewing case studies submitted by signatory companies will be by Warwick University's Corporate Citizenship Unit and staff at MIT, some NGOs have produced their own analyses of the conduct of those companies. The website CorpWatch offered a series of case studies, starting with a study of Aventis, the biotech firm whose Star-Link genetically modified corn was found to have strayed into the food supply. CorpWatch argued that this meant Aventis violated the Global Compact's precautionary principle, which implies that no products should be marketed if effects on health and the environment are unknown. More

UN SECRETARY-GENERAL KOFI ANNAN AND HIGH COMMISSIONER FOR HUMAN RIGHTS MARY ROBINSON: HOSTED A PANEL AT THE WORLD CONFERENCE AGAINST RACISM

gramme. Toyota Motor Corporation was attacked in the US by Rev. Jesse Jackson following an advertisement that was accused of being racially offensive. The funds will add new minority-run dealerships each year and increase spending on minority advertising, job training and community support. The announcement puts flesh on the deal reached between the company and Jackson earlier in the year to avoid a threatened boycott against the car-maker.

case studies are promised in the coming months.[1]

IN ADDITION TO ITS LEARNING ROLE, the Global Compact is also proving to be a mechanism for involving corporations in intergovernmental conferences on social and environmental issues. For example, in August United Nations Secretary-General Kofi Annan and United Nations High Commissioner for Human Rights Mary Robinson hosted a panel at the World Conference Against Racism to discuss the impact of racism and discrimination in the workplace. The dialogue sought to draw attention to private-sector initiatives that promote equality and inclusion in and out of the workplace. Participants included representatives of Volvo Car Corporation, the International Confederation of Free Trade Unions, Eskom (South Africa), Satyam Computer Services (India), the United Nations Environment Programme and the International Labour Organisation.[2] Kofi Annan was 'encouraged by the commitment of Compact participants who have agreed to throw their considerable weight behind the cause of diversity and non-discrimination'.

ONE COMPANY THAT HAD COME UNDER fire on racism and diversity issues announced a $7.8 billion minorities pro-

Climate for change

IN THE HEAT OF JULY IN GERMANY, delegates managed to agree to proceed with the climate-cooling Kyoto Protocol, without the world's biggest polluter, the United States. As the ink was drying, the protocol was already creating heated debate within the business community, especially in large organisations where parent companies and subsidiaries had opposing views. For example, Swedish auto-maker Volvo publicly supported Kyoto while its parent company in the US, Ford, did not. Coca-Cola, like Ford, belongs to the US Council for International Business, which opposed Kyoto. But Coca-Cola's subsidiary in Spain endorsed the treaty. Pedro Antonio Garcia, from the Spanish subsidiary, said, 'You cannot operate if you are against the Kyoto Protocol in a European context. It's the price of entry.'[2]

In the US, Executive Vice President of the National Association of Manufacturers (NAM), Michael Baroody, wrote to George W. Bush, 'thanking' him for his opposition to the agreement. 'On behalf of 14,000 member companies of the NAM—and the 18 million people who make things in America—thank you for your opposition to the Kyoto Protocol on the grounds that it exempts 80 percent of the world and will cause serious harm to the United States.'[3] Baroody made selective use of sta-

---

1 www.corpwatch.org
2 Reports on the preparatory work on diversity are available from www.respecteurope.com.
3 www.nam.org

tistics. He calculates 80% based on population, not total carbon emissions, 25% of which are produced by just 4% of the world's population living in the United States.

When President Bush dismissed the Kyoto climate change treaty as 'fatally flawed', he meant to spare companies such as the members of NAM from paying to control pollution. But, now that about 180 countries have pushed ahead without the US, some American businesses with overseas operations are left wondering if they've missed out on a commercial opportunity. This is because that, under the treaty, companies that reduce their own emissions of greenhouse gases can sell credits to other companies whose emissions are growing. Although criticised by many environmentalists as letting big business off the hook, this new system means that money will be made from reducing carbon emissions.[4]

No wonder, then, that a new initiative established to help companies express their support for the Kyoto Protocol had generated significant support. Signatory companies of Emission55.com 'call on the governments of the world to ensure the entry into force no later than 2002 of the Kyoto Protocol. This will require ratification of the Protocol by at least 55 countries responsible for 55% of the carbon dioxide (CO_2) emissions from industrialised countries.' A diverse range of companies have already signed, including Otto Versand, Ricoh and the Credit Suisse Group.[5]

MEANWHILE, THE WORLD'S LARGEST OIL group, ExxonMobil, which trades as Esso in many European countries, was beginning to show signs of concern over the StopEsso.com campaign. ExxonMobil is considered a big influence on the Bush administration because, critics say, it helped bankroll the Bush presidential race to the White House. The StopEsso.com cam-

paign widened to include Germany, Norway and New Zealand as well as Britain, where it started. While ExxonMobil representative Lauren Kerr stated that the company did not expect a significant impact, a spokesman for Esso UK told *The Guardian* newspaper that they were 'concerned about the boycott'. The newspaper reported that the company was planning a public relations strategy to try to 'win back customers'.[6] Their strategists might want to look at a new survey that found some 80% of adults take corporate citizenship into account when making purchasing decisions, and 70% do so when making investment decisions.[7] As The Body Shop began daubing 'StopEsso' straplines on company trucks, corporate lines were also being drawn.

The problem, of course, is that different people have different social and environmental concerns. In its September issue, the US-based *Sierra* magazine assessed the environmentalists' best choices for green gasoline companies. The article ranked oil and gas companies not just on the climate change issue, but on a range of human rights and environmental commitments and practices. The key issue for *Sierra* was some companies' plans to drill in the Arctic National Wildlife Refuge, leading to BP, Chevron, Phillips Petroleum and, yes, ExxonMobil, being named the 'Dirty Four'.[8] CSR, it seems, is in the eye of the beholder.

Humane resources

IT'S ONE THING TO FOCUS ON CONSUMER and investor concerns; but perhaps equally important is how company staff feel and react to their employer's position and performance on social and environmental issues. *Business Ethics* magazine reported that companies making job offers to prospective employees might find themselves

4 http://c.moreover.com/click/here.pl?e22552438&e=6347
5 www.emission55.com
6 www.guardianunlimited.co.uk/globalwarming/story/0,7369,508478,00.html
7 http://us.hillandknowlton.com
8 www.pirg.org/reports

faced with questions about the firm's environmental commitments. A growing number of employees—nearly 100,000—have signed up to the activist website Ecopledge. com, making a commitment to reject job offers at corporations that 'fail to take specific, positive environmental actions identified by Ecopledge.com researchers'. Among the steps identified are stopping the sale of polluting products, increasing recycling, and ending controversial developments. Companies targeted by Ecopledge include Boise Cascade, BP Amoco, Coca-Cola, Citigroup, DaimlerChrysler, Dell, Disney, Nestlé, PricewaterhouseCoopers, Sprint and Staples.

Further reinforcement of this trend came with publication of the third annual POLLARA survey for the Women's Executive Network which showed that the most important factor attracting women executives to an employer is the organisation's ethical conduct. The organisation, Canada's largest public opinion and marketing research forum, found that women placed ethics ahead of other factors such as the quality of the organisation's leadership, the quality of its products and services, its overall reputation, and remuneration.

SO IT SEEMS THAT MANY PROFESSIONALS do need a purpose for the paycheque. For example, Nick Wright of UBS Warburg, the investment banking division of UBS, told the Warwick Corporate Citizenship Conference that 50% of all applicants asked about corporate citizenship during their interviews. And a survey of 255 UK employees by the Industrial Society found that more than half claimed to have chosen the company they work for because they 'believe in what it does and what it stands for'. Study author Stephanie Draper, head of corporate social responsibility at the society, said a tight UK employment market is putting pressure on companies to become 'employers of choice'. (Despite fears of a recession in the US, the labour market in the West remains tight, especially for highly skilled individuals.) The

findings 'challenge prevailing recruitment and retention strategies which centre on pay and benefits,' she added. 'Other priorities such as ethics and reputation are now playing a more important role.' It is therefore no surprise that Lifeworth.com reported high uptake in its new *CSRJobs Bulletin*, which lists job opportunities in the corporate citizenship field. It reached over 1,000 subscribers within a month of launching its service.[9]

SRI 'R' Us

SOCIALLY RESPONSIBLE INVESTMENT (SRI) research bodies from 12 countries joined forces to provide data on companies' social and environmental performance for institutional investors. The Sustainable Investment Research International (SiRi) group explained that it will offer standardised profiles of the largest 500 global companies as well as SRI consultancy services. SiRi will have a combined total of 100 researchers to draw from, who will focus on environmental performance, employment practices, customer relations, community involvement, governance standards and supply chains. The group spent the previous year standardising the research practices of its members, who will pool their research on companies in the FTSE Eurotop 300 index, Standard & Poor's 100 in the US, and 100 Canadian and Japanese corporations. Each member will continue to research its respective national markets. The partners are: Kinder Lydenberg Domini from the USA, AReSE (France), CentreInfo (Switzerland), Caring Company (Sweden), Scoris (Germany), Triodos Bank (Netherlands), Michael Janzi Associates (Canada), Avanzi (Italy), ECodes (Spain), Stock at Stake (Belgium), the Sustainable Investment Research Institute (Australia) and the Pensions Investment Research Centre (UK). The plan is that they will be joined by a Japanese partner.[10]

---

9 www.lifeworth.com
10 www.sirigroup.org

INDICATIONS THAT INTEREST IN SRI is growing in Japan came when the first Japanese bank signed up to a United Nations statement on sustainable development. By signing the UN Environment Programme (UNEP)'s 'Statement by Financial Institutions on the Environment and Sustainable Development', the Development Bank of Japan (DBJ) committed itself to a 'precautionary approach' to environmental management. The statement, set up in 1992, also requires the state-owned bank to recognise that 'sustainable development depends upon a positive interaction between economic growth and environmental protection'. Most of the 171 financial institutions that have signed to date are European, so UNEP hopes that DBJ's lead will increase the number of Asian signatories. Deputy governor of DBJ, Takashi Matsukawa, said the bank would help UNEP to get other financial institutions in Asia involved.[11]

Efforts such as this, aimed at increasing the profile of SRI in the South are important. Given the limited experience and capacity the South has in this field, it is understandable yet regrettable that no Southern groups are involved in the SiRi initiative at this stage. Although the key financial centres are in the North, most quoted companies have extensive operations in the South, where their positive and negative impacts need to be researched, analysed and prioritised by independent and informed local people. As investors' interest in information that is credible to a broad range of local and global stakeholders grows, so this may become a more serious issue.

Branding criticism

ECHOING CONCERNS FROM LEADERS in the private sector that NGOs are sometimes too quick to condemn companies that begin working on corporate citizenship, a representative of Amnesty International (AI) called on NGOs to give the benefit of the doubt when companies make public statements about their aspirations on human rights. Writing in the third *Visions of Ethical Business*, edited by Warwick Business School's Malcolm McIntosh, AI's business group manager Peter Frankental argued that 'when a company associates itself with values of any kind it is often making a statement of how it wishes to be perceived, rather than of what it actually does'. This, he explained, 'creates a gap between aspirations and reality . . . which causes many NGOs to dismiss aspirational statements as a public relations exercise'. He warned that, if NGOs reject a company's aspirational statements, they risk 'throwing the baby out with the bath water', as before a company can integrate social values into its operations it must develop the aspiration to do so. Considering the importance of corporate reputation and branding, Frankental suggested that 'a company that ties its flag to the mast of human rights is offering a hostage to fortune. If it fails to deliver on its stated commitments, its credibility will be at stake.'[12]

This issue arose at a seminar on corporate power and globalisation hosted by Respect Europe. Delegates from NGOs and corporations discussed how NGOs are often dependent on the media for communicating their message, and that this can affect the way they talk about companies. To be heard, NGOs must 'brand' themselves and their criticisms as much as companies brand themselves and their products or services. Hypocrisy is a better story than mere malpractice, so NGOs and activists may find it easier to attract media attention if they focus on those companies that say they are addressing the issues.[13] This reveals the complexity involved with communicating corporate citizenship policies, and the importance of developing understanding with NGOs.

11 www.unepfi.net
12 www.business-minds.com
13 www.respecteurope.com

The politics of partnership

IN JULY, AUGUST AND SEPTEMBER, A spate of publications appeared that analysed the proliferation of corporate codes of conduct. In a new book from the Carnegie Endowment for International Peace, Virginia Haufler explores codes of conduct across three different policy arenas: environment, labour and information privacy.[14] She identifies the common driving forces for, challenges to and questions from the increasing application of voluntary codes of conduct. In the magazine *Foreign Policy*, an article described an emerging 'NGO–Industrial Complex' constituted by businesses and NGOs working together on ethical codes of conduct and certification.[15] 'While certification will never replace the state, it is quickly becoming a powerful tool for promoting worker rights and protecting the environment in an era of free trade', argue Gary Gereffi, Ronie Garcia-Johnson and Erika Sasser.

The UN Research Institute for Social Development (UNRISD) previously theorised these relationships as forms of 'civil regulation'—the quasi-regulation of business by civil society.[16] It followed up this work with a new report welcoming developments in corporate codes of conduct and certification, but warning of the 'danger that codes may be seen as something more than they really are'. Report author Rhys Jenkins cautions that they 'can be used to deflect criticism and reduce the demand for external regulation. They can also undermine the position of trade unions in the workplace.' He argues 'how vitally important it now is to develop strategies to ensure that codes are complementary to government legislation and provide space for workers to organise'.[17] A new report

funded by the Aspen Institute's Nonprofit Sector Research Fund suggests that NGO involvement in codes of conduct and certification can be challenging and lead to conflict within civil society. The report chronicles both the difficulties and successes faced by Rainforest Alliance in certifying Chiquita Brands International plantations with its Eco-OK scheme.[18]

COLLABORATIVE RELATIONS BETWEEN the private sector, governments and NGOs is the subject of a new report from the World Bank's 'Business Partners for Development' (BPD) project. *Endearing Myths, Enduring Truths* draws on partnership examples in natural resources, water and sanitation, road safety and youth development, to argue that tri-sector partnerships 'benefit the long-term interests of the business sector while meeting the social objectives of civil society and the state by helping to create stable social and financial environments'.[19] The World Bank's BPD is one of a number of organisations promoting the concept of inter-sectoral partnership. In the UK, the International Business Leaders Forum (IBLF) launched the 'Partnership Brokers' website, which is intended to act as a resource for partnership-building.[20] In the US, new specialist agencies have appeared in this field.[21] The Copenhagen Centre is also actively promoting the idea of inter-sectoral partnership.

At the end of June, 400 people from all sectors gathered in Copenhagen to hear Danish Prime Minister Poul Nyrup Rasmussen's speech on 'Partnerships and Social Responsibility in the New Economy'. Mr Rasmussen said that Europe and the European Union is in a 'unique position to take a major step forward in

14 www.ceip.org/pubs
15 www.foreignpolicy.com/issue_julyaug_2001/gereffi.html
16 www.unrisd.org/engindex/media/press/murphy.htm
17 www.unrisd.org/engindex/media/press/jenkins.htm
18 www.jembendell.freeserve.co.uk/GrowingPain.htm
19 www.bpdweb.org/krg/myth_prev.htm
20 www.partnershipbrokers.net
21 See www.collaborationworks.com and www.corcom.org.

DANISH PRIME MINISTER POUL
NYRUP RASMUSSEN: EUROPE IS IN A
UNIQUE POSITION TO MOVE
FORWARD IN IMPLEMENTING
PUBLIC–PRIVATE PARTNERSHIPS

ALTHOUGH MANY WOULD WELCOME such initiatives for IT development, not everyone working on corporate citizenship shares the view that public–private partnerships are *always* desirable. Some are concerned that public–private partnerships can mask the commercialisation of sectors that had hitherto been the preserve of the public sector, such as water, health and education. Julian Liu of the Center for Economic and Social Rights argued in a letter to *The New York Times* that

> international financial institutions and multinational corporations are pushing privatization plans that transform water from a common resource available to all into a commodity for purchase. The result: low-income communities around the world are forced to seek water from polluted and untreated sources, leading to needless deaths from waterborne diseases. For these reasons, international human rights law recognizes the right to water as an essential component of the rights to life and health. Government and business should also recognize that the right to safe drinking water must neither be bought nor sold.

implementing and mainstreaming corporate social responsibility and public–private partnerships'.[22]

These groups advocate that at local, national and international levels partnership-building has emerged as the approach most likely to bring about truly sustainable development. They argue that bridge-building between the public sector, the private sector and civil society is effectively promoting social cohesion, environmental stability and equitable economic growth. Proponents point to projects such as Togo's first Cisco Networking Academy, opened at the University of Lomi in August. That project is part of a global effort by the United Nations Development Programme (UNDP) and Cisco, the leading supplier of computer network routing equipment, to set up Networking Academies in 29 of the world's 49 least-developed countries by the end of 2001. There are now more than 70 innovative international public–private partnerships, according to a recent inventory by the Geneva-based Initiative on Public–Private Partnerships.

THE WORLD HEALTH ORGANISATION (WHO) has also realised the sensitivity around this issue, dedicating the August edition of its *Bulletin* to the question of public–private partnerships for drugs and vaccines.[23] WHO argued that 'partnerships between the public sector and private enterprise can bring wide benefit in terms of improved health, but there must be safeguards to make sure that their prime focus is healthier populations rather than richer companies'. Overcoming just three of the world's biggest killers—tuberculosis, malaria and HIV/AIDS—requires action by both governments and the private sector, according to the *Bulletin* editor-in-chief Richard Feachem. 'Either alone will be insufficient', Feachem warned. Pub-

---

22 www.copenhagencentre.org/tcc2001
23 www.who.org

lic–private partnerships can increase the chances that the biotechnology revolution will benefit not only the rich but also poorer populations, he said, so long as the respective energies and expertise of both sectors are efficiently harnessed to attain their common objectives.

Writing from his experience as chief scientific officer of the Medicines for Malaria Venture, Robert Ridley urged commentators to focus less on the differences between public and private bodies and more on the opportunities that partnerships can offer. The aim, he says, is not 'bargaining to obtain maximum advantage to one side or the other' but 'commitment to a common goal through the joint provision of complementary resources and expertise, and the joint sharing of the risks involved'.

Possible pitfalls in WHO's interaction with industry were highlighted by Yale University's Kent Buse and WHO's Amalin Waxman. For example, could WHO's advocacy functions become subject to commercial pressures, and could the organisation's traditional concern for the poorest and least commercially 'attractive' populations be influenced by partners with necessarily different concerns? To ensure that WHO's involvement in partnerships reflects its constitutional commitment to equity and public accountability, the authors propose, among other things, that WHO's relations with the private sector be based on clear benchmarks of 'good partnership practice'.[24]

The concern raised in *JCC*'s last World Review was where the necessary investment into research for the development of drugs and vaccines for the poorer countries of the world would come from, especially when pharmaceutical companies were slashing their drugs to cost price, due to corporate citizenship considerations. The answer suggested in the *WHO Bulletin* is a combination of factors that provide both 'push' and 'pull'. 'Push' factors include public investment in the basic

EUROPEAN COMMISSION OFFICIAL IN CHARGE OF THE DEVELOPMENT OF EUROPEAN POLICY ON CORPORATE CITIZENSHIP, DOMINIQUE BE: WANTS CORPORATE CITIZENSHIP TO DEVELOP ON A VOLUNTARY BASIS

research required and tax credits to participating companies. 'Pull' factors include offering to extend the validity of patents on products and a prior commitment by the public sector to purchase finished products that meet agreed specifications.

Will EU Require IT?

THE RELATIONSHIP OF CORPORATE citizenship to regulation was the focus of an interview with the European Commission official in charge of the development of European policy on corporate citizenship, Dominique Be. He was reported in the September issue of *Ethical Performance* as saying he wants corporate citizenship to develop on a voluntary basis because this encourages innovation and genuine enthusiasm for the concept. Be drafted the European Commission green paper which defined CSR as 'a concept whereby companies integrate social and environmental concerns in their business operations and in their interaction with

---

24 For further information contact Mr John Maurice, mauricej@who.int, or inf@who.int.

their stakeholders on a voluntary basis'. Therefore the EU would not consider legislating to compel companies to adopt corporate citizenship strategies.[25]

The green paper is a discussion document, and the Commission's thinking is at an early stage. The underlying theme of the green paper is that social responsibility is in everyone's interest, but will be meaningless without rigour and transparency. So companies need to produce reports with sufficiently uniform information to allow comparisons. Also, users of such reports need the assurance of external input and verification to be able to rely on the information presented. Similarly, consumers who want to buy products that have been produced responsibly need a simple, authoritative labelling system. And investors who want to back responsible companies need clear criteria that can be consistently applied. The paper stresses the importance of transparency and dialogue, with the need for developing multi-stakeholder consensus on the way forward.

CONSENSUS MIGHT NOT BE EASY, AS some would argue that the threat of litigation is a key motivating factor for voluntary initiatives. Professor Ralph Steinhardt from George Washington University Law School maintains that *the prospect of litigation* may have accelerated the use of voluntary, marketplace initiatives pertaining to corporate citizenship in human rights.[26] As the co-ordinator of the Voluntary Codes Forum, Kernaghan Webb, suggests, 'there is often a legal element to voluntary initiatives, and a legal framework within which such programs operate'.

Thus the political implications of concepts such as 'public–private partnership' and 'corporate citizenship' as well as the role of legislation began to be discussed on listservs during this period.[27] These discussions suggest that most professionals agree that the growth in corporate citizenship is a *result* of deregulation and privatisation. Some go further and argue that corporate citizenship is an *answer* to deregulation and privatisation, while others question whether it is enough to solve the problems that arise. Some go further still and suggest that corporate citizenship is a *justification* for more deregulation and privatisation, while others argue the importance of good regulation and key public services being provided as a right and not for profit. There is no consensus among professionals working in this area, although some seem to assume so.

ISO wants consistency

WHILE THE EUROPEAN COMMISSION was stressing the need for greater consistency in corporate citizenship terminology and practice, across the Atlantic the US Ethical Officer Association (EOA) was asking the International Organisation for Standardisation (ISO) to consider developing a solution. The EOA represents 400 mainly US-based multinationals, including companies such as GM, Microsoft and Philip Morris. Following in the wake of ISO 9000 (the quality standard) and ISO 14000 (the environmental management standard), proposals are now being drawn up to create a new ISO standard for ethical business conduct. Termed a 'Business Conduct Management Standard' (BCMS) by the EOA, it would focus on management processes rather than ethical outcomes. It would aim to specify the internal structures, processes and resources that would be required to enable a company to be consistent in the implementation of its principles of ethical conduct. One of the arguments used in favour of the proposed standard is that the authority of a verifiable ISO standard would help companies to fend off the competing demands gener-

25 www.ethicalperformance.com
26 www.globaldimensions.net/articles/cr/steinhardt.html
27 For example, corporate-citizenship@yahoogroups.com

ated by a plethora of codes and guidelines.[28]

Some groups working in corporate citizenship may raise questions about the benefit of this proposal. ISO 14001 has been criticised for giving the semblance of environmental quality and consistency when it allows companies to set their own environmental standards and priorities (apart from requiring legal compliance). Therefore an ethical ISO standard could disguise very different ethical performance among certified or registered companies. This is a concern, given the current state of corporate ethical codes that often ignore key issues such as freedom of association and collective bargaining. In addition, some may be concerned that, as ISO standards are suited to large companies who can document complex management systems, so the widespread adoption of BCMS might marginalise already-disadvantaged producers and independently run SMEs (small to medium-sized enterprises).

The EOA's suggestion that the BCMS could be based on a company's self-declaration of commitment and performance may concern many NGOs who have for a number of years advocated the importance of independent verification. Commercial auditing firms, whose ISO 14001 auditing services have proved lucrative in the past five years, may echo their concerns. However, these auditing firms and NGOs may disagree on the appropriate form of independent verification, given the high costs of commercial audits and their current limited expertise on labour rights issues.

In addition, those local NGOs already involved in monitoring factories' codes of conduct may question the legitimacy of ISO, given that its membership is restricted to national standards organisations and that it has developed a methodology for auditor accreditation that is more suited to commercial auditing companies. For example, the Independent Monitoring Working Group (IMWG) has developed a

form of ethical standards monitoring that is predicated on a different methodology to ISO, by involving local NGOs as ongoing monitors, advisors and arbitrators of disputes. In September the IMWG released a report on the history and development of independent factory-monitoring initiatives in El Salvador, Guatemala and Honduras.[29] The initiative started in 1995 when labour problems at the Mandarin International factory in El Salvador became widely reported. Most apparel companies doing business at the factory stopped sourcing their brand-name products from the facility. However, Gap Inc. agreed to stay and explore the creation of an independent factory-monitoring programme in El Salvador. They also agreed to work with the Business for Social Responsibility Education Fund (BSREF), the Interfaith Center on Corporate Responsibility (ICCR) and, later, the Center for Reflection, Education and Action (CREA) towards that goal; and hence the Independent Monitoring Working Group (IMWG) was formed.

In the report, IMWG argues that it has demonstrated that companies and NGOs from Central America and the US can join forces to enhance efforts to respect workers' rights. 'During this five-year collaboration, we have learned a great deal about how different perspectives can enrich efforts to create fair, harmonious and productive working conditions', said Rev. David M. Schilling of the ICCR. In El Salvador, the IMWG engaged four local organisations that formed the original Independent Monitoring Group of El Salvador, or GMIES. The primary objective of monitoring was to promote harmonious and productive working conditions through verifying factory compliance with national labour laws, international conventions and Gap Inc.'s own 'Codes of Vendor Conduct'. The report emphasises the importance of attending to the rights of workers in global supply chains, and providing workers with a new channel through

28 www.eoa.org/BCMS/bcms.html
29 www.iccr.org

which to raise concerns about their treatment and the conditions under which they work. Therefore, they contend that independent monitoring works best when it is joined with effective internal factory systems that allow workers to express their concerns without fear of retaliation. They also argue that an independent monitoring process should provide for a third party to act as intermediary or negotiator, when problems or concerns arise.

This is interesting news for other players in the labour standards monitoring field, such as Social Accountability International (SAI). It shares a similar methodological approach to ISO, accrediting international firms to carry out inspections, and doesn't put the same emphasis as IMWG on continual monitoring, dialogue and mediation at the local level. More information on its approach is contained in the book *SA 8000: The Definitive Guide to the New Social Standard*, which features case studies of companies using the standards.[30] In July, SAI teamed up with the International Textile, Garment and Leather Workers' Federation (ITGLWF) to conduct a workshop in the Philippines. The programme builds on the ITGLWF's network of study circles: factory-based groups that have proven to be very effective for worker education and organising. Over the course of three days, 32 study circle leaders worked with the materials, geared towards promoting worker awareness about globalisation and human rights in the workplace and fostering worker participation in codes of conduct.

WITH THE QUESTION OF RETAILER responsibility for the social and environmental practices along their supply chain now firmly established on the corporate citizenship agenda, a report from Egypt started some retailers thinking 'How low can you go?'. Down the supply chain, that is. Human Rights Watch (HRW) issued a report showing that Egyptian children working in cotton-farming co-operatives

LOIS WHITMAN, EXECUTIVE DIRECTOR OF THE CHILDREN'S RIGHTS DIVISION OF HUMAN RIGHTS WATCH: THE WAY CHILDREN ARE TREATED IN THE COTTON FIELDS IS DEPLORABLE

worked long hours, were routinely beaten by foremen, and were inadequately protected against pesticides and heat exposure. The child labourers, most between the ages of seven and twelve (the country's legal minimum age for seasonal agricultural work), earned an average of three Egyptian pounds (about one US dollar) each day. 'The way children are treated in the cotton fields is deplorable', said Lois Whitman, executive director of the Children's Rights division of HRW. Although retailers might already have thought they were bending over backwards to deal with social and environmental issues involved in the *manufacture and assembly* of their products, it seems there are issues of concern right at the base of the supply chain. Perhaps it is not feasible for retailers to go any lower down the supply chain? Perhaps this is a question of suppliers and governments needing greater capacity to deal with these issues?[31]

International perspectives at Warwick

In July the UK University of Warwick's Corporate Citizenship Unit (CCU) held its

30 www.business-minds.com/detail.asp?item=100000000013532
31 www.hrw.org/reports/2001/egypt

4th annual conference. Delegates from industry, government, civil society organisations and academia flew in from around the globe to discuss the latest news, views and research of people working in collaboration with the CCU.

During the opening plenary, former Assistant Secretary-General Professor John Ruggie shared his thoughts on, and hopes for, the UN Global Compact. Professor Ruggie explained that the Compact would be using its website as a way of showcasing corporate experiences in implementing the nine principles, and facilitating the review of corporate submissions by civil society. He explained that it was a practical and pragmatic decision to focus on encouraging and facilitating changes in corporate practice, as the UN did not have a mandate to directly regulate companies. Therefore, he identified the Learning Forum as 'the heart of the change mechanism' envisaged by the UN Secretary-General's office. Ruggie noted that there are differing opinions on the efficacy of a learning approach in creating positive change, but stressed that the Global Compact was only part of the solution to the problems posed by economic globalisation. He noted a number of the challenges that they will face in future. 'There are some things that a learning model by itself cannot achieve. The Compact's recognition and promotion of a company's "good practices" provides no guarantee that the same company does not engage in "bad" ones elsewhere', he warned. In addition, Ruggie noted the possibility that some companies would seek to join in order to deflect criticism—including that coming from other agencies in the UN system.

In a packed workshop on 'Shared Values and the Global Compact', Dr Malcolm McIntosh expressed the aim to start 'a global conversation' on the role of the corporation. He reported mushrooming interest in the Compact from around the world, because of 'the moral authority of the UN', which gave the principles 'a cer-

MALCOLM MCINTOSH: AIMS TO START 'A GLOBAL CONVERSATION' ON THE ROLE OF THE CORPORATION

tain provenance'. McIntosh explained that the first submissions from corporations were being analysed by members of the Learning Forum and would be posted along with comments from reviewers and selected NGOs over the coming months. He explored the key issues that they would consider when assessing the submissions, noting the complexity of the area and how they would themselves be learning how corporations can operationalise the Compact's principles.[32]

THE SECOND PLENARY FEATURED presentations on recent experiences in South Africa, Burma and Vietnam. Gavin Anderson of the Development Resources Centre in South Africa, stressed that the development challenges faced by his country were so great that individual companies would need to work together to drive positive change. He suggested that corporate citizenship should not be seen as the activity of individual companies but as a collective process. He called for an active 'corporate citizenry' to work together on social and environmental challenges.

Jerry Sternin, of Save the Children USA, excited delegates with his experiences of working in Burma and Vietnam. He intro-

32 www.unglobalcompact.org

duced delegates to the idea of 'positive deviance'. He asserted that 'in communities throughout the world there are a few "deviant" individuals whose uncommon behaviours or practices enable them to outperform or find better solutions to pervasive problems than their neighbours with whom they share the common resource base'. He showed that you could find appropriate solutions to development challenges by identifying the problem and identifying how some 'positive deviants' manage to cope better, and then devising an intervention that allows that deviance to be copied by others. This was essentially a development studies lecture, which was of interest to delegates for two reasons. First, companies are increasingly involved in development work in Southern countries and are hungry for the experiences and ideas of the governmental and voluntary development communities. But they were also interested for a quite different reason: Sternin was describing how to provoke positive behaviour—something that delegates are aiming to do, not so much in the South, but in the boardrooms of corporations. Sternin's theory suggests that more research could be conducted on the positive deviants who are champions of corporate citizenship in the business world. If we can identify what made them take a lead and how, then it might be possible to replicate their positive deviance across the private sector.

Delegates also heard the perspectives of people working on aspects of corporate citizenship in Latin America. Marcello Paladino, of Austral University in Argentina, argued that 'Latin America needs new leaders' and that socially aware business leaders should take on responsibility for the state of Latin society. He stressed that 'enterprises are related to social transformation' and that the values embodied in ethical business are the values that could help their society progress. Emphasising this political dimension to business, he suggested that 'management is a political discipline, as it [business] can't be understood outside the community. Enterprises without the community do not exist.'

ANOTHER WORKSHOP FOCUSED ON the 'Challenges for Development Professionals Working with Business Partners in Zones of Conflict'. In his presentation entitled 'Securing a Licence to Operate in Zones of Conflict', the Vice President for Social Responsibility at the Norwegian oil company Statoil, Geir Westgaard, dealt with the difficult issue of oil companies operating in places such as Burma and the Sudan. He argued that oil companies should not be expected to try to influence the way oil revenues are spent in war-torn areas where they operate. 'There are real limits as to how far beyond the factory gate a corporation can move without jeopardising its licence to operate,' he said. 'Even though the role of the corporate sector has increased significantly with globalisation, business has to be careful about demands that fall outside the scope of legitimate action by a commercial entity.'

As featured in the JCC 3 World Review, some NGOs have called on oil companies such as Talisman to freeze its operations in war-torn countries, where oil revenues not only fund the purchase of arms but are considered to be a key reason why governments wage war against separatist groups. However, Westgaard suggested it was 'highly questionable' whether international oil companies should be telling host governments how to spend their oil revenues—and warned that such moves could easily transform corporate social responsibility into political interference.

Westgaard's depiction of economic activity (oil production) as non-political and political activity (civil war) as non-economic was questioned by some during discussions, especially as there appeared to be an economic motive for the Sudanese government waging civil war. Interestingly, Westgaard's analysis seemed somewhat contrary to the presentation from Richard Jones of Premier Oil, who emphasised how corporate constructive engagement with regimes such as the Burmese military dictatorship could help catalyse change and protect human rights. Jones chronicled Premier's initiatives such as training Burmese security personnel on human rights principles and law, and also intimated that its high-level advocacy efforts might help develop the government's thinking. Perhaps with more dialogue the various opinions on these issues might begin to converge. For example, while Westgaard was reluctant to unilaterally place conditionalities on its investment, he suggested that 'if and when we do . . . it will be as part of a broader effort that involves the international community. The conditionality should then be imposed by legitimate international bodies such as the United Nations . . . with the oil companies cast more in a supporting role.'

After examining the feedback from delegates, the CCU outlined their plans to make the 5th annual conference an opportunity for more dialogue and debate on the issues raised, including different and perhaps more critical stakeholder perspectives.

What does the public think about CSR?

Staying ahead of the curve on CSR...

General Public vs Opinion Leaders in G20 Countries Surveyed (n=20,000)
■ General public   ▨ Opinion Leaders

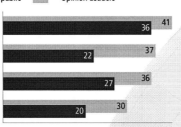

Believe role of companies is to help build better society — 36, 41
Discussed ethical behavior of companies "many times" — 22, 37
Made Investment based on company's social performance — 27, 36
Punished a socially irresponsible company — 20, 30

Research suggests that the attitudes and behavior of opinion leaders may be used to predict the direction of public opinion on emerging issues. Insight from the CSR Monitor reveals that opinion leaders expect more from companies than the general public. Companies are therefore likely to come under greater pressure to deliver on their broader social responsibilities.

The annual **Corporate Social Responsibility Monitor** explores the business case for good corporate citizenship and examines where companies are particularly vulnerable on CSR. Interviewing 20,000 citizens in 20 nations on their changing expectations of companies, the CSR Monitor is essential reading for global corporations wishing to stay ahead of developing social issues which may impact their business.

ENVIRONICS
INTERNATIONAL

Environics International is a leading public opinion research consultancy, specializing in the analysis of global social issues for leading institutions and corporations throughout the world.

For more information or to order your copy, please contact Shannon Stevenson shannon.stevenson@EnvironicsInternational.com
Or visit our website at: www.EnvironicsInternational.com

Introduction

JCC Theme Issue: *Australasian Perspectives on Corporate Citizenship*

David Birch

*Corporate Citizenship Research Unit,
Deakin University, Australia*

IN THE LAST FEW YEARS THERE HAS been a marked increase in interest in issues of corporate citizenship in Australasia and Asia. Some large companies in the region, BP, Rio Tinto, BHP, Shell, Placer Dome, Bristol-Myers Squibb, for example, have taken very decisive moves in developing corporate citizenship programmes and policies. Furthermore, some NGOs, such as World Vision, the World Wide Fund for Nature and the Earthwatch Institute, have recognised the need to become aware of the changing relationships between the corporate world and NGOs because of corporate citizenship debates—moves that were clearly seen at the Second National Conference on Corporate Citizenship held in Melbourne in November 2000 dedicated to business– community partnerships (see Birch 2001c). Also, at some levels of government, federal, state and local, interest, though not necessarily reflected in policy change, has been high. The Business Council of Australia, the Australian Institute of Company Directors and the Australian Prime Minister's Business Community Partnership have all become involved, in one way or another, with some of the issues. Research is growing on a number of fronts with an increasing number of players getting involved: academic, business,

government, NGOs and consultancies (see e.g. King 2000a, 2000b; Centre for Corporate Public Affairs 2000; Business Council of Australia 2001; Armstrong *et al.* 2001; Birch 2001a, 2001b).

But there remains considerable confusion about what exactly constitutes corporate citizenship. For many, especially as expressed in the mainstream media in Australia, corporate citizenship is generally defined as corporate philanthropy: a means of a company 'earning' its licence to operate in a community by virtue of its 'good deeds'.

However, at the First National Conference on Corporate Citizenship in Melbourne in November 1998, organised by the then newly established Corporate Citizenship Research Unit at Deakin University, other definitions emerged. These definitions were more closely linked to sustainability, long-term corporate–community involvement and the powerful concept of the triple bottom line, where the financial, social and environmental bottom lines come together to more strategically define corporate responsibilities beyond the single economic bottom line (see Birch 1999).

What emerged from that conference, apart from the clearly developing interest in all sectors in Australia in the need to engage more fully with corporate citizenship—however defined—was to assess, as much as possible, not so much what individual companies were actually doing in terms of their corporate–community activity, but whether those companies were thinking strategically and long-term about corporate citizenship issues, and, if they were, whether this thinking was being translated into a business case-driven philosophy of corporate cultural change.

A very valuable survey of 115 companies in Australia was commissioned by the Prime Minister's Business Community Partnership and conducted by the Centre for Corporate Public Affairs in 1999/2000, in association with the Business Council of Australia. This survey answered many of the questions about the 'what' of corporate–community involvement—sponsorship, cause-related marketing, business–community partnerships, matched giving schemes, volunteering, *pro bono* work, and so on—activities that, for the most part, have little, or no, effect on long-term corporate culture (see Centre for Corporate Public Affairs 2000). But what was also clearly needed was a much more defined understanding of the level of strategic thinking in the business world in Australia about corporate citizenship and its place in the proactive development of long-term core business, and not simply as a reactive, short-term, 'feel-good' add-on, or marketing/branding device.

Mark Glazebrook, of the Corporate Citizenship Research Unit, carried out a comprehensive study of the annual reports, CEO statements and company publications of the top 500 companies in Australia issued between 1995 and 1999. He found that only 37 of these companies (7% of the 500) actually viewed corporate citizenship as 'central to the strategic direction of their business', as demonstrated through their vision statements, business objectives and overall performance measures for company directors (Glazebrook 1999: 122). Of these 37 companies, 15 had only taken this step in 1999. It was clear from this study that individual companies interpreted corporate

citizenship in different ways, with eight priority areas ranked as follows (Glazebrook 2000: 7):

► Governance

► Ethics

► Sponsorship

► Stakeholders

► Partnerships

► Product stewardship

► Environmental responsibility

► Social responsibility

Valuable though this analysis was, and still is, annual reports and vision statements, in many cases, tend to be aspirational in the more intangible areas of triple-bottom-line and corporate citizenship/responsibility issues, and may not always reflect reality.

In a follow-up study of the top 200 corporates in Australia (see Birch and Batten 2001), the Corporate Citizenship Research Unit at Deakin University explored three main issues:

► The extent to which a company understands the main terms used within corporate citizenship

► The extent to which a company has incorporated the main terms and themes of corporate citizenship into its corporate culture and core business

► The extent to which a company has developed strategic thinking and practices with respect to strategic corporate citizenship and its involvement with the community

The study found that:

► Corporate citizenship is seen by most companies in Australia as being generally synonymous with corporate community activity, and is not perceived as being embedded in the mainstream core business policies and practices of a company, or the way in which the company is organised and run.

▶ Corporate citizenship is generally seen as a short-term community involvement, and a more favoured term for describing this activity was 'corporate social responsibility'.

▶ Corporate citizenship tended not to be mainstreamed with environmental issues in most company cultures and, overall, environmental issues played a much more marginal role in a company's understanding of corporate citizenship than did community involvement, of one sort or another. This signals that there is little ownership of these issues embedded at all levels.

▶ Corporate citizenship, for the most part, was seen to be a top-down process, from the board, the CEO or management, with only a marginal perception that individuals within a company could drive the agenda.

▶ Overall, the agenda of corporate citizenship was seen to be one that always had to answer to the financial bottom line. There was little sense of the mainstreaming of a triple-bottom-line philosophy within companies, despite there being a generally wide acceptance of the need to include social (generally understood rather narrowly as community activities) and environmental issues on a company's agenda—but generally not if this threatened the financial bottom line.

While there is clearly a general commitment to corporate citizenship as expressed in short-term corporate community investment and involvement, this is not, at the moment in corporate Australia, generally managed in a disciplined, transparent and accountable way. The level of public availability of company policies and procedures for community investment, for example, is not high, and the level of published accounts and evaluations very low.

Clearly, these results demonstrate the commitment of corporate Australia, so far,

to an understanding of corporate citizenship as community-oriented involvement, investment and activity, but with significant aspirations towards more long-term corporate citizenship connected to core business and long-term corporate culture. The difficulty facing business in Australia right now is not whether or not they should be involved in community-oriented corporate citizenship, or even, for the most part, whether they should be looking for deeper corporate citizenship roots in their core business activities and strategic thinking. It is how to demonstrate that commitment through actions that make business sense, can be argued through a business case and can be evaluated and measured within the context of growing business in sustainable ways in the future. Significant links have yet to be made by corporate Australia to connect the financial, social and environmental bottom lines, and to inform not only core business, at every level, but to determine how a company is organised and run. What we need to put in place is the vocabulary, indicators and measures that will allow business to do that.

The launch of *The Journal of Corporate Citizenship* is a significant move in this direction, bringing together leading scholars and players in corporate citizenship. This special issue, devoted to Australasian perspectives, is timely in a debate in the region that is gaining momentum every day. Contributors to this issue are leading scholars in the field in Australia, New Zealand and India, and, in the case of Leon Davis, a significant figure in the business community, both in the region and worldwide. These papers cover some of the major issues of corporate social responsibility, stakeholder engagement, corporate governance, corporate social and environmental reporting, corporate community involvement and triple-bottom-line reporting, developed with some very wide-ranging theoretical approaches. This augurs well for the building of strong, conceptual and intellectual foundations on which to build everyday corporate citizenship that will be sustainable for business, government and civil society, both within and beyond Australasia.

References

Armstrong, A., V. Mitchell, G. O'Donovan and M. Sweeney (2001) 'Corporate Social Responsibility: Do Australian banks toe the triple bottom line?', *Journal of Banking and Financial Services* 115.3: 6-10.

Birch, D. (ed.) (1999) *The First National Conference on Corporate Citizenship: A New Research Compact. Proceedings* (Melbourne: Corporate Citizenship Research Unit, Deakin University).

Birch, D. (2001a) 'Business as a Public Culture: Corporate Governance and Development', in A. Mukherjee and D. Reed (eds.), *Corporate Governance and Development* (Calcutta: Oxford University Press, forthcoming).

Birch, D. (2001b) 'Corporate Citizenship: Rethinking Business beyond Corporate Social Responsibility', in J. Andriof and M. McIntosh (eds.), *Perspectives on Corporate Citizenship* (Sheffield, UK: Greenleaf Publishing): 53-65.

Birch, D. (ed.) (2001c) *Proceedings of the Second National Conference on Corporate Citizenship, 16–17 November 2001, Melbourne. Strategic Corporate Citizenship* (Melbourne: Corporate Citizenship Research Unit, Deakin University; Melbourne: Rio Tinto, available from Carolyn Edmonds, ceddie@deakin.edu.au, A$50.00).

Birch, D., and J. Batten (2001) *Corporate Citizenship in Australia* (Melbourne: Corporate Citizenship Research Unit, Deakin University, available from Carolyn Edmonds, ceddie@deakin.edu.au, A$35.00).

Birch, D., and M. Glazebrook (2000) 'Doing Business—Doing Culture: Corporate Citizenship and Community', in S. Rees and S. Wright (eds.), *Human Rights, Corporate Responsibility: A Dialogue* (Annandale, Australia: Pluto Press): 41-52.

Business Council of Australia (2001) *Towards Sustainable Development. How Leading Australian and Global Corporations are Contributing to Sustainable Development* (Melbourne: Business Council of Australia).

Centre for Corporate Public Affairs (2000) *Corporate Community Involvement. Establishing a Business Case* (Melbourne: Centre for Corporate Public Affairs in Association with the Business Council of Australia).

Glazebrook, M. (1999) 'Corporate Citizenship and Action Research: An Australian Perspective', *International Association for Business and Society, Tenth Anniversary Conference Proceedings, Paris* (International Association for Business and Society, www.iabs.net).

Glazebrook, M. (2000) 'Corporate Citizenship in Australia', *The Corporate Citizen* 1.1: 6-11.

King, D. (2000a) *Corporate Citizenship and Reputational Value: The Marketing of Corporate Citizenship* (Adelaide: Hawke Institute, University of South Australia; National Heart Foundation of Australia).

King, D. (2000b) *Stakeholders and Spin Doctors: The Politicization of Corporate Reputations* (Hawke Institute Working Paper Series, 5; Adelaide: University of South Australia).

David Birch is Professor of Communication and Director of the Corporate Citizenship Research Unit, Deakin University, Australia. He has published widely in communication and cultural policy in Asia and is on the editorial boards of several international journals. He is currently working with a large number of companies and organisations in Australia on corporate citizenship, including BP, Rio Tinto, TXU, Worldvision, the City of Melbourne, Ford and BHP.

✉ Corporate Citizenship Research Unit, Deakin University, 221 Burwood Highway, Melbourne, Victoria, Australia 3125

🖥 birchd@deakin.edu.au

Commentary

The Social Responsibility
of Corporations*

Leon A. Davis
Chairman, Westpac Banking Corporation;
Deputy Chairman, Rio Tinto

ONE OF THE FASCINATING QUESTIONS of our time is why, when the free enterprise system has obviously proved its superiority over its rivals, there is so much unease about the social and political consequences of free markets. With the major exception of the United States, those who hold the right-of-centre philosophy are on the defensive almost worldwide and the global businesses that have flourished in the post-war era of freer trade are under increasing criticism.

Why is this when, with the collapse of Communism, they were the obvious winners in the 1990s? Is it because people simply want the reassurance of checks and balances? Or has the wealth created over the last decade or so highlighted the division between those who have participated in this wealth creation and those who have not? Or is it that trade and business has become so big and all-encompassing that it is seen to be answerable to no one?

Through all of this is a common thread—a demand from a broad spectrum of the community that businesses exhibit greater social responsibility. In my view, this feeling is so intense that companies that ignore this aspect of doing business will erode their competitiveness. Indeed, unless the business sector reverses the current perception of blinkered behaviour and arrogance, it can expect increased regulation and a reduction in the public sanction of many business activities.

Both the Prime Minister of Australia, Mr John Howard, and Mr Joseph Elu, in the preceding lectures of this series, emphasised the public's heightened expectations of business. So, in the course of this lecture, I want to do four things.

First, I am going to suggest, very briefly, why many of the current demands made of Australian business are justified. Second, I will describe a business case for activities that might once have seemed inappropriate for the private sector. Third, I will give examples from mining, the industry in which I have spent most of my life, of how the Rio Tinto Group is attempting to give shape and meaning to the term 'corporate social responsibility'. And, fourth, I will suggest that the experience of the global mining companies has lessons for other major Australian enterprises.

---

* Address to the Menzies Research Centre, Melbourne, 18 May 2001.

With power comes responsibility

One reason that more is expected of business these days is that business—and the economy—has benefited a great deal from micro-economic reform in Australia. The reform process allowed Australia to become internationally competitive, in part by reducing the role of government. For the first time business values were allowed to take centre stage and the role of many of the institutions and systems that had underpinned the previous protected mixed economy diminished accordingly.

However, all reforms come at a cost. The previous system resulted in numerous inefficiencies, but the costs of these were widely spread and hard to see. Today we promote transparency, and the costs of making Australia a more competitive economy are more easily identified. When the elaborate systems that provided for social ends through the distribution of resources were dismantled, people knew who to blame. So you could say that business is experiencing the consequences of its own success.

While there is no doubt that micro-economic reform has benefited most Australians, there is no denying the social costs. And it is possible that reforms will be rolled back if business does not recognise that it has acquired expanded responsibilities to match its greater capacity to compete.

The business case for social responsibility

I want to start by simply arguing the business case for socially responsible corporate behaviour. Not, I should add, because the business case is the only—or even the most important—case, but because the debate about corporate social responsibility tends to be dominated by moral and ethical arguments to the point that we can overlook the fact that there is a sound business case as well.

I think it is plain that today socially responsible investment is of increasing concern to portfolio managers, aware that more

and more investors want reassurance that their dividends are not obtained at the expense of the environment, indigenous groups or at a hidden cost to future generations.

In North America and Europe there has been a recent surge of interest in developing indices based on environmental, social or ethical criteria against which institutions can measure the market performance of their funds. The Dow Jones has already lent its name to one and the Financial Times and Stock Exchange (FTSE) is about to launch another.

In addition to these examples from the world of finance, similar examples can be found in the legal area, in risk management, even in human resources because, all things being equal, the most promising business graduates prefer to work for companies with a record for socially responsible behaviour.

Moreover, I firmly believe that the short-term costs of socially responsible behaviour are offset by long-term gains. Let me give you some examples to show that:

▶ Expressions of good corporate citizenship are not all that new.

▶ The rewards for socially responsible behaviour may not be immediate but they do happen.

▶ In this area, as in others, globalisation allows companies to profit from the transfer of international best practice.

From the start of Rio Tinto's open-cut copper mine at Palabora in South Africa in the late 1950s management went to extraordinary lengths to avoid discriminating against black employees when apartheid was official government policy. The company avoided the repugnant official policy of short-term migrant contract labour for black employees by providing married accommodation for permanent employees. Rio Tinto also pioneered the integration of black and white housing in the Phalaborwa township. This was risky, in the political system that existed at that time, but, as a matter of principle, management felt it was a risk worth taking.

In 1996, Palabora decided to extend the life of the mine by another 20 years by converting the open-cut mine to an underground one. We had no problem in seeking this economic gain because Palabora enjoys strong support from the democratically elected Government of South Africa.

Resource companies such as Rio Tinto are unique because development is characterised by high upfront exploration and capital costs, well before any cash flow occurs. Thus, to be in this business one has to be a long-term thinker. More importantly, because mines can be around for a century or more, today's policies can set the mine culture, and its relationships with its neighbours well into the future. Further, because operations are often established in developing countries, such policies must be far-sighted as well as enlightened. Thus, for our people, there is an acceptance of long-term planning for, and commitment to, neighbouring communities.

The benefits of community support are tangible and quantifiable. The example that comes most readily to mind is the different histories of the Marandoo and the Yandicoogina iron ore mines, both developed and managed by Hamersley Iron in the Pilbara in Western Australia.

When the earlier mine, Marandoo, was commissioned in 1994, its planners and builders were applauded for their innovative engineering which set new benchmarks for projects of its kind. Less well known was the concern felt within the company at the cost of the 18-month delay incurred by Aboriginal opposition to development approval.

Subsequent research concluded that the Aboriginal people with affiliations to the Pilbara iron ore province felt deeply that they had been ignored and forgotten in the dramatic development of their homeland. But, as Hamersley learned, during the last decade of the 20th century, the land rights debate had developed to the point where the traditional owners of the Pilbara could exert sufficient influence to delay a mining project, even in resource-conscious Western Australia.

Marandoo was a chastening experience for a mining company that prided itself on behaving legally, ethically and generously. Moreover, the added costs were an affront to the professionalism of Hamersley's management. Having suffered from a too passive approach to community relations, Hamersley set out to rectify matters by establishing strong bonds with its neighbours.

Those bonds weren't built overnight. Yet, by persistence and a willingness to listen and to devote adequate resources to its programmes, Hamersley transformed its relationship with the Aboriginal communities of the Pilbara. The proof lies in the speed with which the second mine, Yandicoogina, was developed in the latter half of the 1990s, after thorough and painstaking negotiations with all those with interests in the land affected by the new mine and its transport corridor. Yandicoogina was commissioned in January 1999, five months ahead of schedule and well under budget, a tribute to a new-found competence in building relationships.

Strategic corporate social responsibility

Let me return to the growing necessity for companies to display a social conscience. Insofar as it is a call for business to obey the moral imperative to behave decently and honourably, I support it wholeheartedly. There are some critics who say that business involvement in community/social matters detracts from the main aim of creating shareholder value. I very much think the opposite: I believe that it builds shareholder value. But I do not believe that it is in the interests of the community, whether spelt with an upper- or a lower-case 'c', for business to simply act as a substitute for government. Government's job is the distribution and indeed redistribution of wealth, and business can never do that.

Business must play to its strengths, conscious of the duty it owes to its owners, employees and other stakeholders; conscious, too, that not only are the strengths and capacities of business and government different but that particular sectors of commerce and industry have characteristic features that ultimately determine their expression of socially responsible behaviour.

In the case of the minerals industry, and based on my knowledge of Rio Tinto's operations, I would say that the broad characteristics that distinguish global mining companies are the self-sufficiency that comes from working in remote areas and their experience with cross-cultural communication. Both characteristics are potentially useful in assisting rural and remote communities in Australia or anywhere else in the world. These are the communities where physical isolation or changing economic circumstances have left people without job options and with a corresponding sense of frustration.

Mining in rural and remote Australia

It seems to me, therefore, that the minerals and energy sector can serve the nation and its stakeholders by the intelligent expression of corporate social responsibility in rural and remote Australia. In so doing it will help to defuse some of that frustration and resentment expressed by the shrinking number of Australians who live outside our cities and major towns. It's a resentment summed up in the journalist's expression 'the angry bush'. I must say that I grew up in the bush and, even then, I resented the advantages that the cities enjoyed. And, even all those years ago, mining companies were trying to do something about it.

In a thousand towns and villages in rural and remote Australia, the future appears increasingly bleak. Jobs, schools, banks, post offices, country hospitals and footy teams: all are disappearing like water holes in an extended drought. People who once saw themselves as the economic backbone of Australia and the embodiment of Australian virtues such as self-reliance and endurance feel their contribution—past, current and potential—is forgotten or unappreciated. They feel betrayed, powerless . . . and angry.

Traditionally the target of this anger has been government, a particularly broad target in a federal system such as ours. Privatisation, deregulation, competition policy, petrol taxes, logging bans, native title claims: these are all seen as manifestations of a lack of interest in the fortunes of people once held up as the quintessential Australians.

The political response is predictable. Traditional allegiances of country people are dissolving and votes are being directed to candidates who appear to embrace 'common sense' nostrums that will restore the balance between town and country. Those candidates appeal to a past when Australia was less buffeted by international business competition and largely insulated from non-European political and intellectual forces.

Today, however, that insulation has been deliberately dismantled, often with the active encouragement of business. So business, especially so-called big business, has been arraigned with government, accused of causing poverty and depopulation in the bush. Large corporations are in the dock with mainstream political parties charged with the destruction of rural society.

Manufacturers who shut formerly protected, unprofitable factories in country towns because Australians prefer cheaper, imported products are pilloried. So too are primary producers whose need for export competitiveness results in leaner operations where one employee produces more than two did five years ago.

Globalisation

Why do city dwellers appear to discount the contribution of rural Australia? Why do arguments that primary producers have been among the first to benefit from the removal of tariffs and the opening of new markets fall on deaf ears?

For many country people the answer is simply summed up in a single word: 'globalisation'. To people in an export industry such as mining, 'globalisation' means opportunity, a chance to compete against the best for the biggest prizes. For the producers of minerals and energy, the technical and political advances that have stimulated world trade have been predominantly benign. In many ways the export nature of Australian resource companies made globalisation an easy concept to grasp.

On balance, I would suggest the world is a more comfortable place because of the interdependence that globalisation encourages between nations. The great ideological confrontation that cast a nuclear shadow over the second half of the 20th century was not resolved by force of arms. It receded before evidence that economic growth flourished more strongly when markets were open.

None of this is to say that globalisation is necessarily a comfortable phenomenon for a small-to-medium economy such as Australia. The nostalgia felt by many for the 'good old days' of a controlled currency, protected manufacturers, cross-subsidisation of infrastructure and services, centralised wage fixing, etc. is understandable. Globalisation makes greater demands on us all, just as it promises greater economic and social dividends for those nations that rise to the challenges.

The main thing to realise about globalisation is that nothing we in Australia can do will reverse it; there is no opting out. Once that fact is faced squarely, the task then becomes one of understanding and dealing with the inevitable social and cultural consequences of major economic change and ensuring that we as a nation have the conditions in place, economic and social, that allow us to participate fully in the global society. But I think we should expose the globalisation debate for the old fraud it really is. This nation has always been global in its thinking, never isolationist. We have always followed and participated in international events from our very start as a nation. Compared with most, if not all, other nations we have great advantages here in our economic, business and social conditions. We can be confident—

must be confident—that we can take our fair share of global growth.

Expectations of business

Those who fear globalisation argue that it will turn Australia into a 'branch-office economy'. This phenomenon happens when Australian companies move onto the international stage and their centre of gravity shifts overseas because that is where they see their commercial advantage. The public perception is that Australia has lost another industrial or commercial icon and that the nation is, accordingly, in some way diminished. It is, if you like, the predicament of the city and the bush moved up a notch. As decisions are made overseas, those who inhabit the countryside feel that their voices become increasingly faint.

We, all of us, need to take issue with this depressing perception. It hinges on the assumption that international corporations are blind to anything but short-term financial returns. Also it assumes that a decision made overseas will somehow be based on different considerations to one made locally. Let me say that the management of reputable international corporations recognise, often before local companies, that it is not enough to focus on financial results to the exclusion of environmental and social outcomes. And corporate decisions will be based on what is best for shareholders and not where the head office happens to be.

Nonetheless, the private sector can make a particular contribution to alleviating the problems of the bush. That response can be considerable because the intelligent expression of corporate social responsibility includes knowing when a contribution is both necessary and decisive. Rio Tinto businesses know too that they can maximise their social contribution by collaborating with governments, statutory authorities, NGOs, academic institutions and community organisations in order to make two and two amount to much more than four.

New competences

Developing an intelligent strategy for the expression of corporate responsibility is one thing; being able to effect that strategy efficiently is something else. In 1995 we in Rio Tinto knew that it was imperative to incorporate new competences into the core of the company's professionalism—new competences that went beyond the traditional economic and technical professions, to include social and cultural expertise.

Today, significant progress has been made. For example, all Rio Tinto operations now produce detailed five-year community plans which contain assessments of the social, economic and cultural characteristics of their host communities. The plans reveal how a particular business consults with local people and sets out programmes, strategies and goals for community relations. Management scrutinises these plans with the same rigour that is applied to other facets of the business. Achievement of these goals ranks equally with all other more traditional goals in judging management performance.

In their Annual Social and Environmental Reports you will find details of how Rio Tinto businesses seek to build long-term relationships. It is our opinion that such relationships do not come just from expressions of goodwill and good intentions. Long-term community relations are the product of an open-eyed approach that defines the fundamental values and aspirations of both parties. Only when these are clear can a productive relationship occur. It is imperative that both sides of a relationship understand the mutual aspect of any expected benefits.

If this seems an excessively pragmatic approach, let me say that it is more than matched by the attitudes of some of Australia's most respected and dynamic indigenous leaders. For instance, Noel Pearson and Joseph Elu both display a similar down-to-earth approach to improving the social and economic conditions of Australia's indigenous communities.

Rio Tinto believes the best way its operations can help to correct rural poverty and disadvantage is by building local capacity and by contributing to the creation of a robust regional economy. By robust, I mean an economy strong enough to survive the eventual closure of the mining operation which, in all probability, was originally the nucleus and engine room of that regional economy. That goal is what aligns all our community relations efforts and it dovetails exactly with what we hear expressed by this generation of Aboriginal leaders.

The Marandoo lesson that I referred to earlier was assimilated throughout Rio Tinto. The period since 1995 has seen a transformation in relations between Rio Tinto and the indigenous inhabitants of Australia.

The transformation started when Rio Tinto publicly acknowledged that Aboriginals had a special connection to the land and that, henceforth, all Rio Tinto businesses would act accordingly. That meant that, in the post-Mabo era, Rio Tinto distanced itself from an exclusive focus on the legal uncertainties that followed the formal recognition of native title. Instead the Group resolved to act in the spirit of the new legislation and to seek accommodation rather than confrontation.

In 1995 Rio Tinto published its Aboriginal and Torres Strait Islander policy. The policy was the product of long and searching discussions held throughout the company. Many Aboriginal organisations were approached for advice. Its keystone is Rio Tinto's recognition of, and respect for, Aboriginal and Torres Strait Islanders.

Since then the story is one of giving practical expression to that policy. Its most obvious outcome has been the conclusion of over 30 agreements with Aboriginal communities across Australia. They relate to greenfield and to brownfield operations, and to mineral exploration. In some cases formal Aboriginal title to the area is established; in others it isn't.

Rio Tinto has signed three Memoranda of Understanding (MOUs) with, respectively, ATSIC (the Aboriginal and Torres Strait Islander Commission); the Department of Education, Training and Youth Affairs; and the Department of Employment, Workplace

Relations and Small Business. These MOUs cover direct employment, traineeships and apprenticeships, the development of joint ventures and the establishment of indigenous small business operators contracting to the mines.

There is no doubt that Rio Tinto sees its main role as improving the economic circumstances of its Aboriginal neighbours where that is what the community wants.

Each business has targets for increasing indigenous employment and training at all levels. Comalco's Weipa bauxite mining operation has, for example, set a target of 35% indigenous employment by 2010.

I should mention, however, that Rio Tinto does not devote all its efforts to its own backyard, as it were. The Rio Tinto Aboriginal Foundation exists to support more general initiatives; the only requirement is that they enhance the status and welfare of Aboriginal and Torres Strait Islanders.

It is a concern among the inhabitants of mining communities in outback Australia that the population of their towns is contracting as mines become more efficient. People note that new mines have increasingly been built with a workforce that commutes by air from a capital city on what is known as a 'fly in, fly out' (FIFO) basis. The worry is that, if the trend continues, those communities will decline below a certain critical point and trigger a loss of services and amenities akin to that experienced in the rural areas.

FIFO certainly makes economic sense in specific instances, and for shorter-lived mines especially. Nevertheless, I have some sympathy with those who say we need to look harder at the social trade-offs involved in this practice.

Yet the real answer to shrinking numbers and the threat that this poses to the continued existence of infrastructure and amenities may well lie in the creation of a stronger regional economy. When Aboriginal communities have great numbers bringing in a pay packet then the future of the school, the medical centre, the post office, the bank, the hotel and the general store is assured. When Aboriginal communities increase their participation in mining—either directly or indirectly—I can see those mining towns taking on a new vitality.

Spreading the message

The Australian minerals industry, because of its export focus and international nature, had a head-start over other sectors of the economy in tackling the issues of corporate social responsibility. Our critics, too, helped us to focus on these issues much sooner. In the 1970s and 1980s many mining companies were at loggerheads with environmentalists and were seen to be the natural opponents of Aboriginal land-owners. It took the industry some time to realise that being a pillar of the Australian economy was no longer enough to win public approval for its activities. But learn it did . . . eventually.

Today I am on the board of Westpac and banks are experiencing similar criticism. Some in banking are surprised that public criticism is becoming more intense when, because of deregulation, banks have been able to provide better services than ever before. And I think that you can identify the same sense of surprise in the senior ranks of other businesses such as pulp and paper, telecommunications, gaming and so on.

So I was particularly interested to read Joseph Elu's remarks about the role that financial service institutions play in redressing the disadvantage of indigenous communities in the United States and Canada. I was especially interested in the collaboration between government and banks in schemes that stimulated local economies and provided employment opportunities. To my knowledge there are no similar schemes in Australia, although Westpac has recently become part of a joint pilot project with Centrelink and DFACS (Department of Family and Community Services) in Alice Springs to assist welfare cheque recipients in dealing with the technicalities of electronic banking and to provide some financial and budgeting education.

Of course, bankers are conscious of their social responsibility. At Westpac it is an integral part of the way we do business and we do know that we need to focus on the needs of Australians in regional Australia. We at Westpac believe that, unless financial institutions expand their view of what constitutes socially responsible behaviour, they will soon lag behind global best practice for their industry. We do not intend to lag behind best practice, if only because to do so invites re-regulation with its associated costs and inefficiencies.

Let me close by reiterating what I said previously about business having acquired greater responsibilities as a result of being given greater freedom. To my mind there is absolutely no doubt about this: it is not going to go away; if anything, those responsibilities are going to grow. I don't think that it is sensible for business to trespass on territory more properly occupied by government, philanthropic or community organisations. But I do think that business can make a considerable difference to the lives of many Australians if it works strategically and in collaboration with existing institutions. Businesses that enter into partnerships with the community, and do so with conviction and professionalism, are going to be seen as modern, responsive and to have a competitive advantage. And investors already know this.

Community as a Stakeholder

Focusing on Corporate Social and Environmental Reporting*

Michelle R. Greenwood
Monash University, Australia

The notion of organisational stakeholders having a claim in corporate social responsibility is implicit in stakeholder theory. The nature of stakeholder relations, however, has been explored only to a limited extent. Further, the nature of specific stakeholder relationships has received little attention. This paper looks at community as an organisational stakeholder, specifically at the nature of the relationship between the community and the organisation. It focuses particularly on community as a stakeholder in social and environmental reporting. Social and environmental reporting is a method employed by many organisations to provide non-financial information about the company to its various stakeholders. First, the question of how stakeholders are identified is addressed. Definitions and typologies of stakeholders are considered. Existing frameworks for understanding stakeholder relationships are then explored. Importantly, not only are the attributes of the stakeholder considered, but also the attributes of the organisation and of the relationship itself. The relationship between the organisation and the community is then constructed. Factors that potentially make up this relationship are identified. A model that postulates the interrelationships between these variables is developed. The potential impact of national culture, particularly in the Australasian region, is considered. Finally, implications for further research are presented.

- Social responsibility
- Stakeholders
- Social and environmental reporting
- Community
- Australia and New Zealand
- Asia

Michelle Greenwood teaches and researches in management ethics and corporate responsibility at Monash University, Australia. Her work has been presented and published internationally and includes *Business Ethics: A European Review, Business and Society Review* and *Journal of Management Studies*.

✉ Department of Management, Box 11e, Monash University, Victoria 3800, Australia

🖥 Michelle.Greenwood@ buseco.monash.edu.au

* The author wishes to thank Christopher Fayers from the School of Geography and Environmental Science, Monash University, for his helpful comments regarding this paper.

STAKEHOLDER THEORY CAME OF AGE WITH THE SEMINAL WORK OF FREEMAN IN the 1980s (Freeman 1984). 'Although almost 15 years on, no one can underestimate this work's effect on the management literature or undervalue its worth today' (Frooman 1999: 192). Stated simply, stakeholder theory is based on the notion that organisations consist of various stakeholders and that they should be managed with these stakeholders in mind. For Freeman (1984) this concept entailed two significant principles. The first is the principle of not harming the rights of an individual. The second is the principle of being responsible for the effects of the organisation's actions. The author notes that both principles must exist in a balance within the modern corporation. Thus, the stakeholder model balances the rights of claimants on the corporation with the consequences of the corporate form.

More recently, debate in stakeholder theory has focused on two areas. First, there are the questions: Who is a stakeholder? How are stakeholder groups identified and what differentiates them? Second, there is the issue of the nature of the relationship between the organisation and the stakeholder, and between the various stakeholders. How do organisations balance the competing interests of the various stakeholders? Do some stakeholder groups take precedence over others? How are groups prioritised? It is a practical reality that managers do not and cannot treat all stakeholders equally. Managers naturally set priorities in how they spend their time, how they allocate resources, and the importance placed on various issues (Mitchell *et al.* 1997).

Social and environmental reporting (SER) can provide an important tool for stakeholder management (Kaptein and Wempe 1998). This can mean different things to different organisations. SER may serve the purpose of minimising risk or adverse effects on the organisation (Brimlow 1997). In contrast, SER may be a means by which organisations can share responsibility with their stakeholders (Kaptein and Wempe 1998). SER can give the organisation the opportunity to be open and transparent to its stakeholders, and to engage its stakeholders in organisational decision-making (Zadek 1998). Measuring and reporting social and environmental performance is integral to the relationship between an organisation and its stakeholders. Thus, investigation of the SER process is a natural means to explore the nature of stakeholder relationships.

This paper examines the dynamics of the relationship between the organisation and a particular stakeholder group: namely, the community. This is done in the context of social and environmental reporting (SER). Importantly, attention is given not only to the attributes of the stakeholder but also to the characteristics of both the organisation and its managers, and to the attributes of the relationships themselves. Initially, literature discussing the definition and typology of stakeholders is considered. Then there is an review of recent work that focuses on the nature of stakeholder relationships. The relationship between organisation and the community is specifically explored. A model describing the influence of the community and in social and environmental reporting is proposed. Finally, the implications of national culture, particularly in the Australasian region, are considered.

Who is a stakeholder?

Stakeholder theory offers a 'maddening list of signals' on how the questions of stakeholder identification can be answered (Mitchell *et al.* 1997). These include: stakeholders identified as primary or secondary; as owners and non-owners of the firm; as owners of capital or owners of less tangible assets; as actors or those acted upon; as those existing in a voluntary or an involuntary relationship with the firm; as right holders, contractors or moral claimants; as resource providers to or dependants of the firm; as risk-takers or influences; and as legal principles to whom agent-managers bear a fiduciary duty (Mitchell *et al.* 1997). Earlier in the development of stakeholder theory the definition of 'stakeholders' was identified as worthy of attention. The suggestion was made that there were two types of definition of stakeholders. The narrow definition included groups that are vital to the survival and success of the organisation (Freeman 1984). The wide definition included any group or individual that can affect or is affected by the corporation (Freeman 1984). The distinction between narrow and wide stakeholder definitions persists in the literature imbued with practical concerns (Mitchell *et al.* 1997). Narrow views are based on the actuality of limited resources, limited time and attention and limited patience of managers for dealing with external constraints. Broad views, in contrast, are based on the reality that companies can be vitally affected by, or can vitally affect, almost anyone. Under this definition the organisation faces a bewilderingly complex set of claims.

The nature of stakeholder relationships

If the task of the organisation is to balance the inevitably competing interests of the various stakeholders, it would appear essential that any stakeholder model should offer a framework to assist in the understanding of the relationships between the organisation and these stakeholders. Freeman (1984) posited that the stakeholder concept could be seen as a wheel in which the firm is the hub of a wheel and the stakeholders are at the ends of the spokes. This conceptualisation assumes that the relationships are dyadic, independent of one another, viewed largely from the firm's vantage point, and defined in terms of actor attributes (Frooman 1999). The idea, however, that not all stakeholders are equal, and that there is a hierarchy of stakeholders, is also apparent in the stakeholder literature (Langtry 1994). Goodpaster (1991), for example, suggested that the relationship between management and non-owner stakeholders, though morally significant, was different from the relationship between management and owners. Many of the classifications of stakeholders imply some sort of hierarchy. Such conceptualisations, however, fail to provide a practical framework or model of organisation–stakeholder relationships.

It has been claimed that little work has been done with respect to the development of specific structures of stakeholder relations (Husted 1998). In fact, a number of existing theoretical frameworks can be applied to the organisation–stakeholder relationship. These frameworks are derived from areas of organisational theory which include power theory, legitimacy, contractual theory, justice theory, network theory, resource-dependency and institutional theory. This paper suggests that these frameworks can be best understood by considering whether they conceive the organisation–stakeholder relationship in terms of stakeholder attributes, organisational attributes and/or in terms of the relationship itself.

Focus on stakeholder attributes

The notion that stakeholders will interact with organisations in a manner based on the stakeholders' social, political or economic power has been prevalent in the literature. Frooman (1999) suggests that most scholars agree that power is an important stakeholder attribute, while Starik (1995, cited in Phillips and Reichart 2000) believes that 'the stakeholder idea has been almost an exclusively political–economic concept'. Power is seen as an attribute of the stakeholder. The difficulty with power as the defining attribute of a stakeholder is that it does not necessarily differentiate between legitimate and illegitimate sources of power—hence the addition of the dimension of legitimacy by some authors (Clarkson 1995; Mitchell *et al.* 1997).

Legitimate stakeholders are identified by the existence of a contract, expressed or implied, between them and the firm according to the firm-as-a-contract view (Donaldson and Preston 1995). Jones (1995) argues that, because the contract is an appropriate metaphor for the relationship between the firm and its stakeholders, the firm can be seen as a nexus of contracts. Rowley (1997: 892) agrees that the stakeholder environment consists of 'a series of multilateral contracts among the stakeholders'. The contractual approach is justified by applying the theory of property rights where 'property' confers a bundle of many types of rights (as compared with the traditional view of property rights which is traditionally used to support exclusive shareholder rights) (Donaldson and Preston 1995). These contracts vary in formality and in specificity. Stakeholders such as community are believed to have loose quasi-contracts with businesses (Donaldson and Preston 1995). For example, the contract between a company and its community could be described as relational, whereas a contract between a firm and its employees, or its shareholders, is formal and specific.

Mitchell *et al.* (1997) draw on existing organisational theories of power and legitimacy, and add a further construct of urgency, to form a model of stakeholder typology. They propose that: 'Stakeholder salience will be positively related to the cumulative number if stakeholder attributes—power, legitimacy, and urgency—are perceived by the managers to be present' (Mitchell *et al.* 1997: 855). Eight stakeholder types, ranging from 'definitive' stakeholders to non-stakeholders, which can be ranked in importance, are described. Mitchell *et al.* note that stakeholder attributes are dynamic and change over time, are subjective rather than objective, and may not be conscious or wilful on behalf of the stakeholder. This model describes the stakeholder relationship in terms of stakeholder attributes (power and legitimacy) and in terms of situational attributes (urgency). It does not, however, focus on attributes of the organisation, the manager or the attributes of the relationship itself.

These models do not depart significantly from Freeman's (1984) hub and spoke, organisation-as-central, conventional model. They present the stakeholder relationship in its strategic, uni-directional form (how the stakeholder can positively or adversely affect the organisation). They focus on characteristics of stakeholders as the variables that affect the organisation–stakeholder relationship. A comprehensive theory of the firm, however, requires not only an explanation of how stakeholders influence organisations, but also how the firms respond to these influences (Rowley 1997). That is, not only do stakeholder characteristics need to be considered, but organisational or managerial attributes need to be considered as well. This has become the focus of more recent research in this area (Agle *et al.* 1999; Greenwood 2001).

Focus on organisational attributes

It is important to consider the attitude or behaviour of the organisation or its managers towards stakeholders. While it is recognised that these are not necessarily one and the same, for the purpose of this discussion they will be considered interchangeable. Most substantive work on stakeholder theories or models identify at least two streams of stakeholder-oriented behaviour. These are variously called social responsiveness and social responsibility (Wartick and Cochran 1985), strategic stakeholder synthesis and new stakeholder synthesis (Goodpaster 1991), and CSR1 and CSR2 (Frederick 1994). For a summary of some of these theories, see Table 1. The commonality between these

Author(s)	Stakeholder orientation				
	Low social responsibility ←————————————→ High social responsibility				
Kohlberg 1969	Pre-conventional		Conventional		Post-conventional
McAdam 1973	Reactive	Defensive		Proactive	Acquiescent
Wartick and Cochran 1985	Social responsiveness			Social responsibility	
Goodpaster 1991	Strategic stakeholder synthesis			New stakeholder synthesis	
Oliver 1991	Manipulate	Defy	Avoid	Compromise	Acquiesce
Frederick 1994	CSR₁			CSR₂	
Logsdon and Yuthas 1997	Managerial prerogative stakeholder theory		Stockholder theory		Stakeholder theory

Table 1 CLASSIFICATIONS OF STAKEHOLDER-ORIENTED BEHAVIOUR

Source: based on Greenwood 2001

models is the suggestion that there are (at least) two distinct attitudes the organisation can adopt towards stakeholders: the organisation takes into account the stakeholder for the good of the firm (the stakeholder as a means to an end); or the organisation takes into account the stakeholder as a matter of principle (the stakeholder as an end in themselves). Donaldson and Preston (1995) classified these typologies as instrumental and normative stakeholder theory, respectively.

Other models describe organisational attitudes towards stakeholders as a range of potential responses (for a summary, see Table 1). Early work into corporate responsibility by McAdam (1973, in Clarkson 1995) identifies a range of possible managerial approaches: fight all the way (reactive); do only what is required (defensive); be progressive (accommodative); or lead the industry (proactive). Oliver (1991) offered a similar typology of organisational responses to external pressures. She described strategies or tactics of active organisational resistance that organisations may exhibit in response to institutional pressures or expectations. In ascending order of resistance,[1] organisations can acquiesce, compromise, avoid, defy or manipulate external influences.

Attitudes towards stakeholders can also be understood as a developmental process. It has been suggested that the moral development of organisations parallels that of individual moral development (Reidenbach and Robin 1991; Logsdon and Yuthas 1997; Malnick 1999). The way an organisation views its goals and relationships with respect to various stakeholders is an indicator of its moral development. Logsdon and Yuthas (1997) have presented a model (see Table 1) that integrates stakeholder orientations with a model of organisational moral development (based on Kohlberg's [1969] theory of individual moral development). They suggest that the early stages of moral development, which are depicted as responding to one's own needs and desires and responding to external influences only to receive rewards and avoid punishment, would be consistent with managerial prerogative stakeholder theory. The next stages of moral development are where external forces, such as peers or societal rules, are not only accepted but also form the basis of decision-making. This is consistent with stockholder theory. An organisation in the final stages of moral development goes beyond industry and legal expectation to emphasise positive duties that actively promote the welfare of stakeholders. Organisations at this level do not view themselves as separate, but as inter-

---

1 Resistance is seen as a manifestation of the organisation's lack of willingness and ability to conform to the institutional environment (Oliver 1991).

connected with their stakeholders. This is consistent with (normative) stakeholder theory.

For the purposes of this paper, organisational or managerial attitude towards stakeholders will be classified as either strategic, legitimising or moral. Strategic refers to the use of stakeholders to promote the self-interest of the firm. Legitimising implies the consideration of stakeholders in order to justify the company's activities. Moral signifies the consideration of stakeholders based on their moral claims.

Focus on relationship attributes

The changing attitude of companies towards their stakeholders will affect the relationship with those stakeholders. The trend in organisations to move from a defensive to a proactive stance brings about a shift in organisation–stakeholder relationships (Kaptein and Wempe 1998). Companies inclined towards acting defensively give a message to the public of 'trust me', suggesting that society should accept that the company is acting in their best interest and not question it or expect proof (Kaptein and Wempe 1998). Those companies that have learned how to deal with criticism often opt for convincing others of the necessity of their actions. The stakeholder demands to be taken into account, and the company is prepared to do so. This relationship is typified by the maxim 'show me' as the company (at least in part) satisfies the stakeholders. Companies that proactively invite their shareholders to contribute and bear their own responsibility in the dilemmas confronting the company show a 'join us' attitude, or 'normative' response to stakeholder demands (Kaptein and Wempe 1998).

The determination of stakeholder salience based on individual attributes and the existence of explicit or implicit contracts with the firm is less important when stakeholder relationships around a particular firm are considered as a whole. Rowley (1997) has used social network theory to construct a theory of stakeholder influences that accommodates multiple, interdependent stakeholder demands, and describes and predicts how organisations respond to the simultaneous influence of multiple stakeholders. Two structural characteristics of an organisation's network of relationships—density of the network and centrality of the firm in the network—are used to describe four categories of organisational response (see Table 2). The density of the whole network is measured as a ratio of existing number of ties compared with the possible number of ties in the network. The centrality of the firm, or any other actor, refers to the position of the firm relative to other actors.

The discussion to date has drawn on various theoretical frameworks to develop a concept of the relationship between organisations and their stakeholders. Focus is now

Table 2 A NETWORK THEORY OF STAKEHOLDER RELATIONSHIPS
Source: based on Rowley 1997

	High centrality	Low centrality
High density	Both stakeholders and the firm have power and can influence each other.	The firm is vulnerable to stakeholder influences.
Low density	Organisation can stifle stakeholder influences through impeding information.	The organisation is isolated from stakeholders and avoids stakeholder influences.

turned to a specific stakeholder relationship and to the construction of the relationship, between the 'community' and the organisation.

Community as a stakeholder

Stakeholder groups, which fit within the narrow definition of stakeholders discussed earlier, have the advantage of being more readily identifiable as a group. Likewise their needs are more easily noted than stakeholders defined in the broad sense. The exception to this, however, is the stakeholder group identified as community. Community is commonly placed within the narrow scope of the stakeholder groups, yet community as an organisational stakeholder is perhaps the most difficult of (narrow) stakeholder groups to identify and discuss. The question of who we mean by community is complex. Business leaders have variously defined community as local or as global, as potential or actual employees or customers, as government or as environment (Greenwood 2001). Community is potentially made up of a number of other stakeholder groups including employees, customers, unions, pressure groups and environment. It is, however, more than just a sum of the groups. Phillips and Reichart (2000) note that it is notoriously difficult to aggregate communal interests. Furthermore, individuals may hold a variety of different interests and these may be represented through various stakeholder groups. For example, a manager may hold claims on an organisation as an employee, as an owner (by owning shares in the company), as a member of the local community (by living in the area) and as an advocate for the environment (by personal conviction). Thus, there is the likelihood of having one individual represented by a multitude of stakeholder groups (Phillips and Reichart 2000).

Despite a lack of clarification on the nature of 'community' and its values and interests, it is axiomatic that communities are organisational stakeholders. From both an instrumental and a normative stakeholder perspective, it can be argued that the organisation and its managers have an obligation to consider the needs, interests and concerns of their community. Among these interests are likely to be a concern for the health and integrity of their natural environment. Thus, the organisation is obliged to consider community as a stakeholder in its environmental management (Phillips and Reichart 2000).

The impact of community on the broader ethical concerns of the organisation has received little attention in the literature (Bourne and Snead 1999). Prior research into external determinants of organisational ethical culture has focused on both the industry and the national (macro) culture in which the company operates. Community can be seen as a micro-culture that may have an impact on firms' ethical decisions and perspectives. In this sense, community is seen as a holder of distinct values and ethical standards. The role of professional associations as holders of core values on behalf of the community is well established, but these groups are only part of the overall picture. Many professional groups are not specific or diligent regarding the enforcement of ethical guidelines and, further, these professions only constitute a minority of most workforces. Initial research has confirmed the existence of a unique, community-based micro-culture that moderates the culture of organisations (Bourne and Snead 1999). The nature of this relationship and how it is affected by factors within the community (geographic region, size and age of the community, income levels, industry concentration, ethnicity and migration patterns) and by factors within the organisation (organisational size, structure, age, industry and workforce profile) requires further exploration (Bourne and Snead 1999).

Community as a stakeholder in social and environmental reporting

The involvement of community as a stakeholder in an organisation's social and environmental practices is likely to be determined by the amount and level of information available to members of the community and vice versa. Indeed, it is argued that the level of trust between a firm and the members of the community may be a function of the information asymmetry between them regarding environmental practices (Kulkarni 2000). Kulkarni (2000) identifies several reasons, related to organisational structure and processes, why a community may not have full knowledge of a firm's environmental practices. It may be because the information regarding products or processes is considered competitively important or is subject to patents. It is evident that a company is likely to have information regarding new products or processes before the community (and that this time-lag may be extensive). Further, where the manufacturing knowledge is highly technical, information regarding environmental impact will be available to the firm before the community.

Another, more significant, organisational factor that may contribute to the community's lack of information about social and environmental practices is the firm's desire to act opportunistically.[2] Opportunism implies 'seeking self-interest with guile' and is considered, in many ways, to be the opposite of trust (Kulkarni 2000: 218). Such opportunistic behaviour can manifest in the withholding of information, particularly the omission of environmentally sensitive information, or in the manipulation or distortion of information. On the other hand, one of the key ways in which a firm shows that it can be 'trusted' is by provision of environmental information through practices such as environmental reporting. Thus the variation in organisations' attitude towards stakeholders, as discussed earlier, has serious consequences for SER. Reporting serves a different function for different companies depending on their stakeholder orientation. For the 'trust us' company, reporting is a way of minimising community concern. SER provides a smokescreen to discourage stakeholders from further investigation. For the 'join us' company, reporting is not a public relationship exercise presented to convince the public that the company is doing a good job. The purpose of SER for such a company is to share dilemmas with the stakeholders. This requires a vulnerable position for the company and a commitment from the stakeholders (Kaptein and Wempe 1998).

Community, as noted earlier, is not homogeneous. As such it is likely that different segments of the community will have differing information at any one time. The information available to various segments of the community is argued to be a function of the group's attributes including the concern, or perceived concern of the group for the environment, and the resources available to them (Kulkarni 2000). For example, individuals in the lower socioeconomic strata, with limited income and resources, may place priority on basic needs such as employment and housing rather than on information about environmental needs. The interaction between concern for the environment and the resources available is evident. Communities that are perceived as not having high levels of environmental concern or resources are likely to be subject to environmental discrimination (Kulkarni 2000). The presence of pressure groups in the community, in contrast, is a major influence on SER (Tilt 1994). In a study of 59 Australian community lobby groups, Tilt (1994) found that 91% of the groups were engaged in lobbying companies either indirectly (54%) or directly (37%) with respect to SER.

Likewise, social and environment information is not consistent in quality and content. Information about a firm's environmental practices may be gained from a number

---

2 One should not discount the possibility of community groups also acting in an opportunistic manner (Kulkarni 2000).

of different sources both within and outside the company. Information may be gained openly and in good faith, surreptitiously, or even by force. Conflict between an organisation and community groups may in part be a product of the parties obtaining different 'facts' about the firm's social and environmental performance. Pressure groups have definite viewpoints about the amount (quantity) and credibility (quality) of reporting (Tilt 1994). Tilt (1994) concluded that, for Australian pressure groups, a preferred model of corporate social and environmental report would be prepared (or certified by) an external party to prevent bias, omission of important or 'bad news' events, and to improve credibility. The format of the report would be a combination of descriptive and statistical data and would include information on all related interests and subsidiaries of the parent company. The report would be contained in the company annual report, would be supplemented by other policy statements, and would be available to the public or interested parties. These features are consistent with the model developed by the UK-based Institute for Social and Ethical Accountability (ISEA). The process of the development of international standards for social and ethical accounting has been occurring for several years. As part of this process, eight 'quality principles' have been developed and tested. The principles suggested to promote accurate, rigorous and valuable audits are: inclusivity, comparability, completeness, regularity and evolution, embeddedness, communication, external verification and continuous improvement (Zadek 1998; see Box 1).

One might expect companies to differ in how they express their ethical interests. Nicholson (1994) suggests a dynamic interplay between three forms: expressive forms, at the level of espoused concepts and beliefs, which may have the character of rhetoric and ideology (such as mission statements); voluntary action, specific behaviours and communication acts directed at specific groups and issues (such as social and environ-

Box 1 QUALITY PRINCIPLES FOR SOCIAL AND ETHICAL AUDITING DEVELOPED
BY THE INSTITUTE FOR SOCIAL AND ETHICAL ACCOUNTABILITY (ISEA)
Source: Zadek 1998

1. **Inclusivity.** Audits must include and reflect the values and objectives of all stakeholders. The audit must be a two-way process: a 'dialogue' rather than a 'consultation' with the stakeholders.

2. **Comparability.** The audit must allow for the results to be compared with either the same organisation for a different period, or with external organisations as part of a benchmarking process.

3. **Completeness.** The audit must include the full range of the company's relevant activities. This is in order to ensure that the company is not picking the areas of activity likely to yield most positive results. In practice, not every stakeholder can be included, but all stakeholders should be sampled. No area of the company should be deliberately excluded.

4. **Regularity and evolution.** The auditing process should not be a one-off. It should be an ongoing process, occurring regularly and changing over time. These changes should reflect the changes in the organisation and in the composition and expectation of the stakeholders.

5. **Embeddedness.** The auditing process should be designed into the working processes of the organisation. Organisational procedures, its operationalisation of policies and commitments, should allow for regular assessment.

6. **Communication.** The audit must be communicated (not just published) to appropriate stakeholder groups. This may or may not include public disclosure; however, it is likely to include groups external to the organisation such as suppliers and customers.

7. **Externally verified.** The audit should be externally verified as a means of validating the results. The external verification process should be of 'high professional quality and independence'.

8. **Continuous improvement.** The aim of the audit is to assess and contribute to substantive progress rather than to reveal retrospective performance. As such the auditing process should be able to identify changes over time and be linked to methods that promote improvement.

mental reporting); and instituted forms, organisational structures that substantiate ethical interest and intent (such as an affirmative action programme). Considered as a continuum, these forms parallel the easily decoupled (not integrated with organisational practices) to highly integrated ethics practices continuum posited by Weaver *et al.* (1999). Social and environmental reporting itself can be described as varying along such a continuum. Minimal selective reporting, which is carried out as a one-off exercise by an isolated function within the organisation, would clearly be an easily decoupled practice. In contrast, social and ethical reporting, which is part of the ongoing dialogue between many parts of the organisation and various stakeholders, and which affects the way the organisation carries out its ongoing activities on a day-to-day basis (a form measurement for continuous improvement), would be a highly integrated practice. The model of SER as developed by ISEA and others is in keeping with a highly integrated practice. It would be expected that companies that hold a more proactive stance towards their stakeholders would be committed to SER as a highly integrated practice and those taking a defensive stance would engage in easily decoupled SER.

It would appear that a number of different factors might influence the role that community plays in SER. These include: the amount, type and quality of information available to the community; characteristics of the community such as level of concern, resources available, co-ordination and co-operation; the attitude of the company towards its stakeholders; and the processes employed by the company to manage these stakeholders.

Determinants of community involvement in reporting

This paper has sought to develop a concept of the community–organisation relationship in the context of social and environmental reporting. The analysis to this point has revealed a number of features that may influence the involvement of community as a stakeholder in SER. Further, it is proposed that in many cases these features are inter-related and in some cases overlap. These factors, and the possible relationship between them, are depicted in Figure 1.

First, the orientation of the company towards community is significant. The argument that organisations will vary in their attitude towards stakeholders along a continuum from defensive (the stakeholder considered only as an impediment to be overcome) to proactive (the stakeholder seen as a partner with legitimate rights) has been made earlier. The three organisational strategies that are referred to are moral, legitimising and strategic. Second, the nature of the community itself will be a factor in its ability to influence SER. The perceived power and legitimacy of the community or its various groups, and the co-ordination and communication between these groups, will have bearing on the community's impact. These two features will in turn affect the third feature, the actual relationship between the organisation and the community. The community will be affected by the nature of the relationship (characterised by openness, honesty and trust) and by the structures and processes to support communication and co-operation. Thus, the organisational structure and processes for SER, the fourth factor, will also affect the ability of community to influence the practice of SER. The role of the community in SER will be influenced by factors such as whether the company has a consultation process, provides site visits or employs a community liaison officer. In addition, the nature of SER practices (highly integrated or easily decoupled from other organisational practices) will be important. The resulting accessibility and quality of information available to the community is the fifth factor determining the community's influence. The type of information (site reports, impact statements), the method of

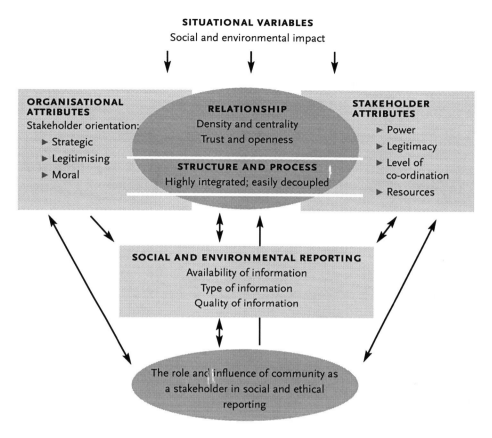

Figure 1 A MODEL OF COMMUNITY INFLUENCE ON SOCIAL AND ENVIRONMENTAL REPORTING

dissemination (web-based, multiple hard copies), the inclusion in the reporting process (consultation, site visits) and the quality of the information (transparency, verification process) will all have an impact on the community's involvement and attitude towards SER.

Finally, there is the situational variable of the extent to which the community is affected by the company's activities. This was referred to as 'urgency' by Mitchell *et al.* (1997). Specific factors may include the geographical proximity of the operations to the community, and the actual and perceived social and environmental impacts of the operations. Situational variables may have an impact on stakeholder attributes, organisational attributes and the relationship itself, thereby influencing the role of community in the SER process.

The impact of culture: focus on Australasia

Social and environmental reporting to stakeholders is dominated by European and North American countries (Zadek 1998). In its recent report on social and environmental reporting, the United Nations Environment Programme (UNEP) scored over 200 companies on their SER practices (UNEP 2001). Of the top 50 companies showing 'best practice' in SER, 27 companies originated in Europe (UNEP 2001: 3). It would appear that European companies followed by North American companies are the main proponents of SER. Australia and New Zealand, despite low populations, also produced three reports in the top 15 (UNEP 2001: 10).

In contrast, Asian countries (with the exception of Japan) did not score highly in their reporting practices (UNEP 2001). Within Asia, the focus tends to be exclusively on environmental reporting and 'stakeholder engagement is conspicuous by its absence' (UNEP 2001: 42). This finding is consistent with the 1997 report of Transparency International,[3] which scores countries across a range of criteria to produce its Corruption Perception Index (CPI). Most Asian countries ranked significantly lower (for example: Taiwan, 31; Malaysia, 32; South Korea, 34; Thailand, 39; Indonesia, 46) than Australia (8), New Zealand (4) and Northern European countries (Denmark, 1; Finland, 2; Sweden, 3; Netherlands, 6) (Grace and Cohen 1998: 205).

This raises the possibility that SER—and, more generally, stakeholder management—may have a tendency to fit with some national cultures and not with others. There is a paucity of research considering the relationship between national culture and social responsibility in general (Maignan 2001), let alone SER in particular. Yet there is ample evidence that national cultures vary and that a variety of management practices differ by national culture (Newman and Nollen 1996). Hofstede's (1980, 1991) five work-related dimensions can be used to identify differences in national cultures from the Australasian region:

▶ Power distance is the extent to which people believe power and status are distributed unequally and accept an unequal distribution of power as the proper way for social systems to be organised (Hofstede 1980). Companies high in power distance, such as those in East Asia, tend to be more centralised and have less (stakeholder) participation in decision-making (Newman and Nollen 1996).

▶ Uncertainty avoidance is the extent to which people are threatened by uncertain, unknown or unstructured situations (Hofstede 1980).

▶ Individualism–collectivism is the extent to which identity is derived from the self versus collectivity. Individual cultures are loosely coupled and status derives from individual accomplishment. Collective cultures rely on membership in groups for identity and status (Newman and Nollen 1996). The Anglo countries of the UK, Australia, New Zealand, Ireland, Canada and the US are very individualistic cultures (see Table 3). East Asian countries such as Taiwan, Korea, Singapore and Hong Kong are highly collective cultures (Newman and Nollen 1996).

▶ Masculine–femininity is the extent to which societal values are characterised by assertiveness and materialism. Femininity is an attribute that reflects the emphasis placed on relationships and concern for others. Masculine cultures include Japan, the Philippines, the US and Australia (Hofstede 1980) (see Table 3). Feminine countries are typified by Nordic countries such as Denmark, Norway and Sweden (Newman and Nollen 1996).

▶ Long-term versus short-term time orientation was added subsequently in an effort to capture dimensions that might be particularly relevant to Asia (Newman and Nollen 1996). Long-term cultures are characterised by patience, perseverance, a

---

3 Transparency International was founded in 1993 to work against international corruption. Part of its mission is to promote transparency and accountability in public administration and international business (Grace and Cohen 1998: 204).

Profile	Individualism–collectivism	Power distance	Uncertainty avoidance	Masculinity–femininity
Stakeholder management*	Collective	Small	Low	Weak
Australia	Individual	Small	Moderate	Strong
Hong Kong	Collective	Large	Low	Strong/moderate
Japan	Collective	Large/moderate	Strong	Strong
New Zealand	Individual	Small	Low/moderate	Strong/moderate
Philippines	Collective	Large	Low/moderate	Strong
Singapore	Collective	Large	Low	Moderate
Taiwan	Collective	Large/moderate	Strong/moderate	Moderate
Thailand	Collective	Large	Strong/moderate	Weak

* This profile is proposed in this paper.

Table 3 CULTURAL PROFILES
Source: based on Hofstede 1980

sense of obedience and a duty towards the larger good (Hofstede 1991). Long-term countries are found in Asia, including Hong Kong, Singapore, Taiwan and Japan (Newman and Nollen 1996).

Intuitively, it would seem that an organisation at the 'join us' level of stakeholder engagement (stakeholder management) would have the particular profile of cultural characteristics. Thus it is proposed that stakeholder management would be characterised by a culture profile of low power distance, low uncertainty avoidance, high collectivism, strong femininity and long-term orientation (see Table 3). In addition to having an impact on organisational attributes (managerial practices and attitudes), national culture may affect stakeholder attributes (community characteristics such as level of concern, co-operation and resources). As such, other dimensions of the relationship model (see Fig. 1) may be affected. The possibility of situational variables (such as economic imperatives) overriding the other dimensions should be also considered.

This construct of culture is limited because it assumes culture is homogeneous and static. There is no mechanism for discussing diversity within a culture, or cultural change. To more fully understand the cultural specificity of SER, further research that comprehensively explores various dimensions of culture in SER and locates these dimensions in an appropriate sociopolitical context would be both necessary and valuable.

Conclusion and future research

This paper has explored the dynamics involved with community as a stakeholder in the organisation, specifically in social and environmental reporting. A number of factors that may influence this stakeholder relationship have been identified. These dimensions have been classified as organisational characteristics, stakeholder characteristics, and attributes of the stakeholder relationship or situational variables. A model of how these dimensions may interrelate has been developed. This model was derived from substantial theoretical frameworks and some empirical studies in both the stakeholder and SER fields of research. This model is only an early stage in the investigation of the community–organisation stakeholder relationship. It is clear that both theoretical and empirical research is needed to continue to develop these suppositions.

In considering the actual performance of companies in the engagement of stakeholders in the SER processes, it would appear that some types of company perform better. Regional differences seem to dominate. Australia and New Zealand perform well; however, countries in Asia (with the exception of Japan) do not. A possible explanation for this is that national culture may match a 'cultural profile' of stakeholder management to a greater or lesser extent. In pursuing this idea it is important that national culture is not seen as homogeneous or static, and that other potentially significant variables are not overlooked. Nevertheless, the potential for the cultural specificity of stakeholder management is worthy of further exploration.

References

Agle, B.R., R.K. Mitchell and J.A. Sonnenfeld (1999) 'Who Matters to CEOs? An Investigation of Attributes and Salience, Corporate Performance, and CEO Values', *Academy of Management Journal* 42.5: 507-25.

Bourne, S., and J.D. Snead (1999) 'Environmental Determinants of Organizational Ethical Climate: A Community Perspective', *Journal of Business Ethics* 21: 283-90.

Brimlow, R.W. (1997) 'Just Do It: Deniability and Renegades', *Journal of Business Ethics* 16.1: 1-5.

Clarkson, M. (1995) 'A Stakeholder Framework for Analyzing and Evaluating Corporations', *Academy of Management Review* 20.1: 92-112.

Donaldson, T., and L.E. Preston (1995) 'The Stakeholder Theory of the Corporation: Concepts, Evidence and Implications', *Academy of Management Review* 20.1: 65-91.

Frederick, W.C. (1994) 'From CSR to CSR 2: The Maturing of Business-and-Society Thought', *Business and Society* 33: 150-64.

Freeman, R.E. (1984) *Strategic Management: A Stakeholder Approach* (Boston, MA: Pitman).

Frooman, J. (1999) 'Stakeholder Influence Strategies', *Academy of Management Review* 24.2: 191-210.

Goodpaster, K.E. (1991) 'Business Ethics and Stakeholder Analysis', *Business Ethics Quarterly* 1.1: 53-73.

Grace, D., and S. Cohen (1998) *Business Ethics: Australian Problems and Cases* (Melbourne: Oxford University Press).

Greenwood, M.R. (2001) 'The Importance of Stakeholders According to Business Leaders', *Business and Society Review* 106.1: 29-49.

Hofstede, G. (1980) *Culture's Consequences* (Beverly Hills, CA: Sage).

Hofstede, G. (1991) *Culture and Organizations* (London: McGraw–Hill).

Husted, B.W. (1998) 'Organisational Justice and the Management of Stakeholder Relations', *Journal of Business Ethics* 17.6: 643-51.

Jones, T.M. (1995) 'Instrumental Stakeholder Theory: A Synthesis of Ethics and Economics', *Academy of Management Review* 20.2: 404-37.

Kaptein, M., and J. Wempe (1998) 'The Ethics Report: A Means of Sharing Responsibility', *Business Ethics: A European Review* 7.3: 131-39.

Kohlberg, L. (1969) 'Stage and Sequence: The Cognitive-Developmental Approach to Socialization', in D.A. Goslin (ed.), *Handbook of Socialization Theory* (Chicago: Rand McNally): 347-480.

Kulkarni, S.P. (2000) 'Environmental Ethics and Information Asymmetry among Organizational Stakeholders', *Journal of Business Ethics* 27: 215-28.

Langtry, B. (1994) 'Stakeholders and the Moral Responsibilities of Business', *Business Ethics Quarterly* 4: 431-33.

Logsdon, J.M., and K. Yuthas (1997) 'Corporate Social Performance, Stakeholder Orientation, and Organisational Moral Development', *Journal of Business Ethics* 16.12–13: 1213-26.

Maignan, I. (2001) 'Consumers' Perceptions of Corporate Social Responsibilities: A Cross-Cultural Comparison', *Journal of Business Ethics* 30.1: 57-72.

Malnick, T. (1999) *Visions of Corporate Responsibility* (British Academy of Management Annual Conference; Manchester, UK: Manchester Metropolitan University).

Mitchell, R.K., B.R. Agle and D.J. Wood (1997) 'Towards a Theory of Stakeholder Identification and Salience: Defining the Principle of Who and What Really Counts', *Academy of Management Review* 22.4: 853-86.

Newman, K.L., and S.D. Nollen (1996) 'Culture and Congruence: The Fit between Management Practices and National Culture', *Journal of International Studies* 27.4: 753-79.

Nicholson, N. (1994) 'Ethics in Organizations: A Framework for Theory and Research', *Journal of Business Ethics* 13.8: 581-96.

Oliver, C. (1991) 'Strategic Responses to Institutional Processes', *Academy of Management Review* 16.1: 145-79.

Phillips, R.A., and J. Reichart (2000) 'The Environment as a Stakeholder? A Fairness-Based Approach', *Journal of Business Ethics* 23.2: 185-97.

Reidenbach, R.E., and D.P. Robin (1991) 'A Conceptual Model of Moral Development', *Journal of Business Ethics* 10.4: 273-85.

Rowley, T.J. (1997) 'Moving beyond Dyadic Ties: A Network of Stakeholder Influences', *Academy of Management Review* 22.4: 887-910.

Tilt, C.A. (1994) 'The Influence of External Pressure Groups on Corporate Social Disclosure: Some Empirical Evidence', *Accounting, Auditing and Accountability Journal* 7.4: 47-73.

UNEP (United Nations Environment Programme) (2001) *The Global Reporters* (Paris: UNEP).

Wartick, S.L., and P.L. Cochran (1985) 'The Evolution of the Corporate Social Performance Model', *Academy of Management Review* 10.4: 758-69.

Weaver, G.R., L.K. Trevino and P.L. Cochran (1999) 'Integrated and Decoupled Corporate Social Performance: Management Commitments, External Pressures and Corporate Ethics Practices', *Academy of Management Journal* 42.5: 539-52.

Zadek, S. (1998) 'Balancing Performance, Ethics and Accountability', *Journal of Business Ethics* 17.13: 1421-41.

AVAILABLE NOW

FULL DETAILS AND DOWNLOADABLE INTRODUCTION AT WWW.GREENLEAF-PUBLISHING.COM/CATALOGUE/CORPCIT

Perspectives on Corporate Citizenship

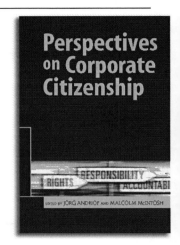

EDITED BY JÖRG ANDRIOF AND MALCOLM McINTOSH

Warwick Business School, UK,   Warwick Business School, UK
and KPMG, Germany

332 pp   234 × 156 mm   Hardback   ISBN 1 874719 39 X   £40.00   US$75.00

A number of disparate but interconnected forces such as deregulation and globalisation, rapid advances in communications technology and the rise in the power of the consumer and civil society have now combined to bring corporate responsibility to prominence in many corporate boardrooms. In this information age, the ramifications of not addressing best practice in environment, workplace, marketplace and community could range from bad press coverage to complete market exclusion. These are perilous times for the social construct of modern capitalism.

In today's society successful companies will increasingly be those that recognise that they have responsibilities to a range of stakeholders that go beyond compliance with the law. If in the past the focus was on enhancing shareholder value, now it is on engaging stakeholders for long-term value creation. This does not mean that shareholders are not important, or that profitability is not vital to business success, but that in order to survive and be profitable a company must engage with a range of stakeholders whose views may vary greatly. If in the past corporate social responsibility was simply seen as profitability plus compliance plus philanthropy, now responsible corporate citizenship means companies being more aware of and understanding the societies in which they operate. This means senior executives and managers being able to deal with a wide range of issues including greater accountability, human rights abuses, sustainability strategies, corporate governance codes, workplace ethics, stakeholder consultation and management.

The aim and scope of *Perspectives on Corporate Citizenship* is to help capture and distil these and other emerging trends in terms of content, context and processes, in one concise volume. With contributions from the crème de la crème of leading thinkers from around the world, *Perspectives on Corporate Citizenship* will become essential reading for students, scholars and all serious thinkers on one of the most critical issues of our time.

❝ This is an impressive collection of the latest thinking in the rapidly evolving field of corporate citizenship. ❞

Jeremy Nicholls
BP Global Social Investment

❝ This book is a fruitful contribution to the emerging international discussion on corporate citizenship. ❞

Prof. Dr André Habisch
Catholic University of Eichstätt

❝ The book brings together an excellent range of material . . . and ought to help companies avoiding some major mistakes. ❞

Dr David Brown
Arthur D. Little Ltd

❝ . . . this book is an essential companion to any person involved in corporate citizenship issues. ❞

Dr Miles Watkins
Aggregate Industries

Orders should be sent to: Greenleaf Publishing, Aizlewood Business Centre, Aizlewood's Mill, Nursery Street, Sheffield S3 8GG, UK.
Tel: +44 114 282 3475   Fax: +44 114 282 3476
E-mail: sales@greenleaf-publishing.com

Or order from our website: www.greenleaf-publishing.com

The Implementation of OECD Corporate Governance Principles in Post-Crisis Asia

Justin Iu and Jonathan Batten
Deakin University, Australia

The recent OECD Principles on Corporate Governance provide a framework for the convergence of global corporate governance practice. This paper considers the implementation of these global 'best-practice' standards of governance as part of the continuing post-economic-crisis reform throughout Asia. These initiatives have explicitly acknowledged that no single model of governance can exist, and instead have focused on those elements apparently common and, therefore, applicable to all countries. Notwithstanding the existence of these elements, this paper investigates the difficulties involved when attempting to implement general rules across countries at different stages of economic and legal development. While implementation will be hindered by obvious cultural disparities, long-term change in practice requires a cultural shift in the philosophical and financial bases of the firm.

- Global corporate governance convergence
- OECD Principles of Corporate Governance
- Post-crisis Asia
- Cultural influences
- Evolution of governance and law
- Ownership structure
- Relationship-based business

Justin Iu is a tutor in finance at Deakin University. He is editor of Amnesty International Australia corporate responsibility newsletter.

Deakin University, School of Accounting and Finance, 221 Burwood Hwy, Burwood, Victoria 3125, Australia

iu@deakin.edu.au

Jonathan Batten is a Professor of Finance at Deakin University. He is an associate editor of the *International Review of Financial Analysis* and the *Journal of Business in Developing Nations*.

Deakin University, School of Accounting and Finance, 221 Burwood Hwy, Burwood, Victoria 3125, Australia

jabatten@deakin.edu.au

www.deakin.edu.au/fac_buslaw/acc_fin/

THE ASIAN ECONOMIC CRISIS HAS EXPOSED CRITICAL DEFICIENCIES IN financial systems throughout Asia. The principal focus of post-crisis research has attempted to link these deficiencies to specific causes such as over-leveraged domestic financial markets, overexposure to foreign exchange risks and monopolistic market structures.[1] Underlying all these issues is a fundamental lack of control. Poor corporate governance is indicative of this problem. Indeed, 'corporate governance provides at least as convincing an explanation . . . as any or all of the usual macroeconomic arguments' (Wong 2000).

The perceived inadequacy of Asian governance models has evoked calls for the introduction of Western-style systems.[2] The 1998 Organisation for Economic Co-operation and Development (OECD) Principles of Corporate Governance—primarily based on Western legal and ethical concepts—represent one such system and 'focus on governance issues that result from the separation of ownership and control' (OECD 1999). In adopting this focus, the OECD Principles acknowledge the trend of incorporating the role of the wider stakeholder group as well as providing for the conventional board (of directors) function in mitigating agency issues.

Importantly, the OECD Principles recognise that governance forms part of a wider macroeconomic context where the legal and institutional frameworks play a major part. The Principles provide for the participation of both governments and the private sector in the development of good governance; these are, to a certain extent, interdependent.[3] It is believed that the basic principles exude commonality applicable across nations. However, due to significant cultural and social differences between developing Asian and Western economies, it is clear that difficulties will arise in their implementation. Furthermore, historically, the contrasting legal, financial and institutional structures among Asian countries has led to the variations in existing governance models. Before the OECD Principles can be effectively implemented, these facts must be accommodated in the reform process.

The objective of this paper is to assess the extent to which cultural factors will affect the implementation of the OECD Principles in Asia generally, though emphasis will be placed on applications in Indonesia, Korea, Thailand, Malaysia and the Philippines. The focus will be on the effects of ownership concentration on shareholder rights, particularly concerning voting rights; the role of relationship-based commercial activity, especially between banks and corporations, and its impact on creditor participation within the governance system; and, finally, the effect of culture on disclosure, transparency and enforcement.

It is imperative that these issues are addressed as part of the ongoing post-crisis reform process. Therefore, this study will identify areas of cultural resistance and, by doing so, assist with the success of future implementation. We argue that, by first understanding the existing laws and the attitudes that created them, policy-makers will be better equipped to adjust Asian governance systems. It is hoped that identification of the areas where difficulty may arise will allow attention to be focused on these areas and provide the means for lasting implementation and change.

---

1 Alternative research suggests the causes may be asset bubble bursting. See Krugman 1998 and Allen 2000.
2 The term 'Western' as used in this paper, represents mainly the law of the United States and the United Kingdom and other English Common Law countries such as Australia and New Zealand. A distinction must be made between civil law countries, in particular those in Europe such as Germany and Italy.
3 Specifically, 'the principles are primarily intended to provide assistance to governments as they pursue their own efforts to evaluate and improve the legal, institutional and regulatory framework that affects corporate governance'. The drive for global governance is premised on the fact the Principles transcend legal and cultural barriers. In particular, 'the report recognises the complexity of the very concept of corporate governance and therefore focuses on the principles on which it is based' (OECD 1999).

The paper is set out as follows. In the next section a review of the relevant literature is provided while the third section establishes the key propositions to be investigated. The propositions are based on the need to correct the Asian corporate governance problem and are formally stated as: (i) the evolutionary concept of governance and law prevents the transplant of the OECD principles; (ii) ownership structure, as representative of culture, will affect minority shareholder protection in Asia; (iii) the role of relationship-based business will affect the participation of stakeholders in the governance system; (iv) the prevalence of insiders in current governance systems will affect compliance with increased disclosure and transparency regulations; and (v) contextual change will assist in the implementation of improved, but not global, standards. Conclusions are presented in the final section.

Literature review

Berle and Means (1932) observed that a consequence of the separation of ownership and management was ownership dispersion and that such dispersion made subsequent monitoring and discipline of management difficult. The heritage of modern governance can be attributed to this observation. Likewise, Jensen and Meckling (1976) developed their concept of agency theory on the separation of ownership and management. Agency theory[4] contends that the inability to properly monitor management allows the existence of opportunistic behaviour.

Corporate governance developed as a way of ensuring that investors receive a return on their investment by protecting against management expropriation or use of the investment capital to finance poor projects. Specifically, 'corporate governance deals with the ways in which suppliers of finance to corporations assure themselves of getting a return on their investment' (Shleifer and Vishy 1997: 737). However, the inability to create perfect contracts, as Hart (1995) suggests, necessitates the need for corporate governance. That is, corporate governance issues arise wherever contracts are incomplete and agency problems exist.

This fact is clearly evident from the empirical investigation of corporate failures during the 1980s, with corporate governance proposed as a general prescription. Various investigative reports suggested the development of codes,[5] although these recommendations were questioned because the costs appeared to place onerous restrictions on smaller firms compared with the benefits they would receive. While initially the primacy of the board of directors remained firmly entrenched in the governance literature, more recently there has been an increasing awareness that an intricate set of relationships, both internal and external, affect the way corporations are governed.

Parallel to the development of these studies has been the development of a comparative literature which identifies a best model of governance based on 'specified attributes' (Gilson 2000: 1). In the pursuit of classification, these 'taxonomists' have focused on the governance systems of the US, Germany and Japan (Shleifer and Vishy 1997; Hopt *et al.* 1998; Rubach and Sebora 1998). For example, Rubach and Sebora (1998) note that the governance responses of the US and Japan differ according to two forms of investor protection. They found the US model, characterised by transparency, better enabled

---

4 Agency theory can be traced to Coase (1937).
5 The codes were initiated following the corporate collapses of the 1980s. The first real prescriptive code was the UK Cadbury Committee Code of Best Practice 1992; recently, the Turnbull Report (1999) finalised code work in the UK. Notable others include the Treadway Commission (USA) and Bosch (Australia). Country-specific undertakings continue in contemporary governance but their terms of reference are often cast wider than the first generation.

investors to monitor corporations, whereas the Japanese model emphasised the development of long-term relationships. Nestor and Thompson (1999) conclude similarly but describe the difference as that between 'insider' and 'outsider' systems. The Japanese–American dichotomy is analogous to the disparity between Asian and OECD Principles.

A recent series of papers by La Porta *et al.* (1998, 2000a, 2000b) compared a larger set of countries, including a number from the Asia–Pacific region. The focus of these studies was the relationship between legal origin, investor protection and finance. La Porta *et al.* investigated these mechanisms as representative of corporate governance regimes. Their findings suggest that investor protection varies depending on a country's legal regime (where investor protection consists of legal protection and ownership concentration). Specifically, common law countries have greater legal protection, whereas civil law countries have higher ownership concentration. Thus, where legal protection is insufficient, countries are likely to have concentrated ownership for protection. Shleifer and Vishy (1997: 769) suggest 'that both the legal protection of investors and some form of concentrated ownership are essential elements of a good corporate governance system . . . [l]egal protection and large investors are complementary in an effective corporate governance system'.

More pertinent to this paper is the recent study commissioned by the Asian Development Bank (ADB) (2000b) to investigate the corporate governance structures of the Asian crisis economies. In the comprehensive analysis, drawn from five individual case studies of Indonesia, Korea, Malaysia, Thailand and the Philippines, the ADB provided a comparison of governance structures, focusing on ownership, finance and control. They found, on the whole, that the governance structures of the crisis economies closely resembled each other. Generally, the elements were high ownership concentration (allowing insiders to dominate control), bank-centric financial systems, ineffective shareholders' rights and low transparency.

Another key issue in the corporate governance literature concerns the convergence of corporate governance systems as part of recent corporate trends towards internationalisation and globalisation. The urgency of post-crisis reform, however, necessitates that the protracted course of improvement through natural convergence be replaced by a more expedient method. As a result, the introduction of a Western system of governance has been proposed. Convergence towards this path has primarily been supported through the efforts of international organisations. Thus, there is an increased resolve to implement global corporate governance standards. This indicates convergence of practice is most desirable.

Given the signs of convergence mentioned above, the concept of global standards is not totally inconceivable. Indeed, Nestor and Thompson (1999) observe that 'despite different starting points, a trend towards convergence of corporate governance regimes has been developing in recent years'. However, Heuer *et al.* (1999) identified that 'a recurring theme in national culture research is that while convergence may be seen in practices among managers, these practices "do not necessarily signal a convergence in the values embedded in national cultures"'. The difficulty is encapsulated in Scott's comment on the wider nature of governance which 'bring[s] in the social and cultural norms of society' (Jordan 1999: 1) as affecting the nature of governance.[6] This prevents lasting change. Economic liberalisation has provided the illusion of a world in which past barriers have been removed and also a world in which nations are becoming more similar. The conduct of commerce between nations on homogeneous terms and conditions does not translate into homogeneous cultural constructs. National identities

---

6 These difficulties will be related to literature documenting legal transplants and the concept of nontransferability below (Mattei; Montesquei, etc).

remain. Cultural differences also remain. Thus, the 'starting points' become the major impediment to implementing the selected international standards: the OECD Principles of Corporate Governance.

So, while post-crisis reform has already made significant changes to corporate governance, to apply a term often used in Western commercial law, when one 'lifts the corporate veil' it is revealed that the fundamental nature of governance has changed little. In terms of corporate governance, the difficulty in changing existing systems comes from the concept of path-dependency. Rubach and Sebora (1998: 2) find 'differences in corporate governance systems reflect the paths by which each came to exist'. Bebchuk and Roe (1999: 127) argue that path-dependencies 'may freeze the institutions of particular countries in a noncompetitive pose'. Caution is equally pertinent to the Asian context. Jordan (1999: 5), too, notes that the dangers raised by using the OECD Principles in Asia could force the production of ineffective change. Similarly, Allen (2000) argues that, if the Principles are transplanted immediately, not much will occur in the short or even mid-term.

From the convergence literature above, it becomes apparent that each country's path to good governance will be different. Indeed, the quest for 'convergence does not mean that corporate governance reform will be implemented identically in each country' (ACGC 2000: 2). For the purpose of this paper, however, discussion was initially premised on the notion that correcting Asian corporate governance would follow this course. A more detailed analysis has revealed that the major codes and official documents have all acknowledged that no single model of corporate governance can be applied that will adequately solve the governance issues in every situation (see ADB 1995, 1999, 2000a, 2000b; IMF 1999; OECD 1999; World Bank 1999). Instead, these studies maintain that good governance should be developed on a contextual basis because the specific circumstance of each country (let alone each corporation) differs. For example, the ADB states, 'each country should formulate its own reform plan and implement measures that suit its specific conditions' (ADB 2000a: 6).

Notwithstanding the allowance for individual development to meet particular circumstances, the international benchmark will still encounter some difficulty in implementation. The source of this difficulty can be traced to the fact that many of the concepts included in the good governance model are founded on Western ideals. What is needed is a solution geared to the specific problem; no path is the same. If a successful solution is desired, it must be framed in Asia. The following section investigates these issues within the context of specific propositions.

Development of key propositions

Post-crisis reform is well under way throughout Asia, though significant work remains. Where does the challenge begin? The OECD sees the need for the 'observance of environmental and social standards' in reform (OECD 1999: 23). Thus, it becomes apparent that the difficulty of reform lies not in the development of adequate standards but in their actual implementation. The implementation challenge can be summarised in one word: culture. Despite the claims of universal applicability of governance principles, implementation will be affected by cultural factors. Hence, the primary proposition investigated is that cultural idiosyncrasies will cause resistance to change and ultimately affect implementation. This paper focuses on ownership structure and insider relationships as representative of cultural resistance. We suggest five propositions which shall be discussed in turn: (i) the evolutionary concept of governance and law prevents the transplant of the OECD principles; (ii) ownership structure, as representative of culture, will affect minority shareholder protection in Asia; (iii) the role of relationship-based business will affect the participation of stakeholders in the governance system; (iv) the prevalence of insiders in current governance systems will affect compliance with increased disclosure and transparency regulations; and (v) contextual change will assist in the implementation of improved, but not global, standards.

Proposition one: the evolutionary concept of governance and law prevents the transplant of the OECD Principles in Asia.

The urgency of reform has evoked appeals for the correction of poor corporate governance to be accomplished by introducing Western governance standards—specifically, the replacement of existing systems in Asia with the OECD Principles. This procedure resembles legal transplanting. A legal transplant is essentially the process of transferring a system of law that was developed in one country to another country. The concept of a legal transplant appears straightforward. Indeed, the mechanical process of replacing one law with another is relatively simple. However, this theory fails to account for practical issues that follow: namely, the application of transplanted laws by the constituents of receiving countries. It is argued that laws evolve out of an organic process. This concept is drawn from the 'rule of non-transferability of law', which contends that effective legal transplants are unattainable, as the development of law should be evolutionary in nature.[7]

Given cultural differences between jurisdictions, concepts may not be interpreted with the same effect as originally intended. In reviewing comparative law research, Alston finds that it is often concluded that 'the prospects of foreign legal transplants succeeding in soil which has not been meticulously prepared over a lengthy period of time are minimal' (Alston 1999). The danger, therefore, is that the fundamental characteristics, values and intentions of the original law are lost in the transfer, if interpreted without reference to the underlying context. Similarly, Berglof and von Thadden (1999: 5) see the implications from transplants as being 'particularly uncontroversial for developing countries . . . where laws are likely to be the weakest'. These conclusions are the exception and not the rule. Rather, the evolutionary concept of law is the norm.

Thus, 'lessons derived from the experience of any one country or group of countries, regardless of how successful it or they have been, cannot be transplanted directly' (ADB 1995: 15). Indeed, Jordan (1999: 5) documented the consensus arising from an Asian Corporate Governance Roundtable that 'indiscriminately mixing and matching concepts from different legal traditions, also risks producing legislation that is ineffective, ignored or distortion producing. Asia is littered with past mistakes of this kind.' Therefore, the evolutionary concept of law supports the position that the aim of implementing global governance standards is problematic.

An alternative argument sees that, throughout much of Asia's legal history, law preceded economic development, but economic development was an important condition for the acceptance of laws. This means that, as reform cannot be delayed, implementing the governance changes now is considered prudent—even if they are without immediate effect or full compliance in the short term—in the hope that, when they are needed, society will utilise them. The result is change on a long-term horizon.

The discussion thus far has considered law to be separate from governance. However, the law itself is crucial to good governance. The fundamental nature of law is reflected in the World Bank statement, 'corporate governance is concerned with the systems of law and practice which will promote enterprise and ensure accountability' (World Bank

---

7 The preamble to the OECD Principles recognises that they are evolutionary in nature.

Group 1999: 3). La Porta *et al.* (2000a: 5) see the law as 'one of the principal remedies to agency problems' and that governance is a function of legal protection. Specific laws and their relationship with specific propositions will be discussed in later propositions.

Concluding, culture underlies most of the difficulties with transplants. The implication for the OECD becomes: while beliefs that universal laws should transcend societal influences, there is a general consensus that law is inextricably linked to cultural values. Indeed, Nestor and Thompson (1999) believe culture transcends legal regimes. The remaining propositions investigate the effect of culture on specific governance changes.

Proposition two: ownership structure, as representative of culture, will affect minority shareholder protection in Asia—OECD Principles I and II.

Perhaps the one concept most representative of cultural difference is ownership structure, and ownership structure in turn determines the governance problem. This proposition deals directly with the influence of ownership structure on the implementation of the OECD Principles in Asia, focusing on the relationship between ownership structure and OECD Principles I and II: the rights and equitable treatment of shareholders.

The two key features of corporate ownership structure are concentration and composition. Asian firms are perceived to be highly concentrated, family-dominated corporations (Claessens *et al.* 1999, 2000). It is possible to determine the nature of the agency problem by the degree of dispersion between management and ownership. High dispersion (low concentration) occurs when the majority of ownership is held by a large number of individual, minority shareholders. The problem then is that between management and minority shareholders. Low dispersion (high concentration) is where the majority of ownership is controlled by a small number of large shareholders. The problem then is between majority and minority shareholders.

From Table 1 it is clear that the primary crisis economies all have concentrated ownership. On average, the five largest shareholders, combined, own 55% of each firm in crisis economies. Indonesia, with 67%, is the largest and Korea, with 38%, the lowest concentration. Thus, with low ownership dispersion the agency problem arises between majority and minority shareholders.

The second part of ownership structure is its composition. Ownership composition essentially means who owns the corporation—who the shareholders are. Examples of shareholders include individuals, a family or family group, a holding company, a bank, an institutional investor or a non-financial corporation (ADB 2000b: 7). Importantly for governance, it must be determined if any owners form a controlling group(s). Table 1 also provides information on the composition of Asian corporations. From it, we can see that Asia consists primarily of family-based ownership. There is a tentative link between composition and concentration. That is, it may be credible to assume that ownership composition is a result of ownership concentration because corporations are often established by founding families.

Wallich, in the case of the Philippines, showed that just ten families virtually held control of over half the Philippines' corporate sector in terms of market capitalisation, and such control 'bred a culture of cross shareholdings, absence of independent directors, related-party lending and evasion of single borrower limits' (Arceo-Dumlao 2000a). According to a World Bank study, only Indonesian ownership concentration was higher, with majority shareholders controlling 61.7% of all corporations (Arceo-Dumlao 2000b). Collectively, these findings suggest that Asian corporations are predominantly concentrated, family-based and with a controlling majority. Shleifer and Vishy (1997: 754-55) concur, stating that 'heavily concentrated share holdings and a predominance of controlling ownership seems to be the rule'.

	Korea	Indonesia	Malaysia	Philippines	Thailand
Number of public corporations (1998)	345	178	238	120	167
Percentage of corporations under family control*	24	67	42	46	51
Average ownership (%) of the five largest shareholders per firm†	38	67	58	60	56
Ownership (%) of the ten largest firms (market capitalisation)‡	23	53	46	56	44

* ADB 2000b: 26
† ADB 2000b: 22
‡ Nam et al. 1999: 13

In researching data on ownership concentration in Asia, it became apparent that no two studies could provide the same results. This is (as Nam et al. [1999] also note) because of the difficulty in defini-tively determining ownership structures from the information available. Thus, the figures provided are approximate, taking into account all studies cited. Furthermore, the table represents only publicly listed corporations. It is fair to assume that the concentrated ownership figures presented here would increase dramatically if privately held firms were included in the data set.

Table 1 OWNERSHIP CONCENTRATION IN ASIA

Under these circumstances the protection of investors is a fundamental objective. In countries where developed capital markets exist and ownership is predominantly dispersed, investors can rely on legal protection. However, in other less financially mature markets, legal protection is often inadequate. Unfortunately, Asian financial markets are not well developed (Johnson et al. 2000). In this case, La Porta et al. (2000b) see concentrated ownership assuming a positive monitoring role, substituting for poor legal protection. In fact, they observe that ownership concentration reflects weaker legal protection. Often the financial leverage provided by investment can overcome failings in law and judiciary, as protection can be achieved with little need for court assistance (Shleifer and Vishy 1997: 753-54). Thus, La Porta et al. (2000b) identify ownership concentration as an important element of corporate governance, especially its role in monitoring. The form of concentration dealt with is the large institutional investor. While a powerful tool, institutional monitoring is not directly pertinent to this discus-sion. Instead, the ability of minority investors to form concentrated ownership groups to protect their respective interests is considered.

The ADB (2000b: 6) finds that, in 'East Asian countries . . . where corporate owner-ship is concentrated, corporate management is usually in the hands of controlling shareholders'. Indeed, Dyck (2000: 29) comments, in the case of family controlling shareholders, 'the distinction between owners and managers is eliminated in most cases'. Using the Claessens et al. sample for East Asia, Dyck calculates that family controlling shareholders directly participate in management 67% of the time. Given this link, protecting minority shareholders from the abuse of controlling shareholders becomes the fundamental problem.

In fact, regardless of the type of ownership structure, there will always be the funda-mental risk of large shareholders redistributing wealth for self-interest that is not necessarily congruent with other stakeholders.[8] However, given the fact that many Asian corporations are family-based, the investors in this case are particularly susceptible to abuse. The existence of family-dominated corporations presents substantial impediments to increased minority rights. The ability to participate is a function of shareholder rights, protection of those rights and exercising the rights. The OECD Principles suggest increasing this ability.

Essentially, when granting shareholder rights, the control already held by existing parties becomes a problem, especially when we consider the number of shares held by the respective parties. In the context of family ownership concentration, that means, by its nature, these shareholders will hold a majority of shares. Therefore, increasing minority rights (apart from minority oppression provisions, not discussed here) will have little effect, as family members will still hold control. From Table 1 we see that on average the degree of family ownership concentration in the Asian crisis economies exceeds 55%.

Proposition three: the role of relationship-based business will affect the participation of stakeholders in the governance system—OECD Principle III.

The concept of stakeholders is consistent with the wider view of corporate governance. As mentioned above, while maintaining the shareholder maximisation principle of modern corporate finance, many other stakeholders exist and need to be accounted for. Stakeholders possess a powerful ability to influence corporate behaviour and decisions. OECD Principle III, 'The role of stakeholders in corporate governance', recognises the potential influence of stakeholders and encourages their active participation in corporate governance. These relationships are most evident in the financing relationships of Asian firms.

Most Asian capital markets are undeveloped, with the provision of external corporate finance dominated by banks. Table 2 provides information on the size of bank lending and equity market capitalisation in the crisis economies for 1997. Clearly, the dependence on bank finance over equity is shown. Indonesia and Thailand (60.2%/21.7% and 125.5%/23.0%, respectively) appear to have a greater dependency than Korea, Malaysia and the Philippines (47.6%/16.9%, 165.8%/132.3% and 72.3%/51.7%, respectively). The economic effect of the Asian Economic Crisis was compounded by the bank-centric nature of many Asian economies.

This extant bank–corporation relationship can be used as an example of the possible influence of culture. It is the principal factor that has dissuaded the development of equity as a source of finance. Simply stated, the use of equity dilutes the control of members as it expands the ownership base. The perpetuation of bank financing in this circumstance becomes clear: the choice is made because it protects control. In addition, family members will also jostle with each other for control, using banks to limit the dilution of power and control in a similar fashion to protecting the dilution of control to outside investors. This internal conflict arises from family succession problems (Berglof and von Thadden 1999; Batten and Kim 2000). The ADB finds that 'widespread excessive borrowing . . . could be a symptom of the . . . drive to increase the capital under their control without simultaneously reducing their ownership share' (ADB 2000b: 33). Alternatively, Berglof and von Thadden (1999) note a justification of the choice is the 'presumption . . . [that] external finance really constrains growth'.

Generally speaking, relationship-based commercial activity is the result of cultural tendency for group affiliation. This is especially true of Asian nations. Perhaps the most

---

8 This manifests in several forms: straightforward expropriation, inefficient expropriation or incentive effects on other stakeholders.

	Outstanding bank loans	Equity market capitalisation
Indonesia	60.2	21.7
Republic of Korea	47.6	16.9
Malaysia	165.8	132.3
Philippines	72.3	51.7
Thailand	125.5	23.0

Table 2 BANK LOANS AND EQUITIES IN ASIAN CRISIS ECONOMIES IN 1997 (% OF GDP)
Source: ADB 1999

indicative of deficient Asian commercial relationships is the so-called 'crony capitalism'. Here, the relationship between business and government is close and is used to obtain financial favour (Berglof and von Thadden 1999: 23). The concept is equally pertinent to other corporate relationships. 'Corporate governance is affected by the relationships among participants in the governance system' (OECD 1999: 3). The lack of prudential supervision allowed the perpetuation of a relationship-based banking environment where lending decisions were more heavily influenced by personal affiliations than by merit.[9]

Thus, the predominant governance problem in developing nations is related investors. 'A problem associated with banks being significant shareholders of non-financial corporations is that they may become soft in granting loans. This derives from the conflict of interest that may arise when banks are both owner and creditor' (ADB 2000b: 7). 'In some cases, the fact that creditors (banks or non-bank financial institutions) are parts of conglomerates distorts incentives of lenders to discipline borrowers and undermines their role in monitoring' (ADB 2000b: 41). 'Companies are sometimes interconnected through ownership or other business relationships with their creditors, which is a further obstacle for creditors to take legal action against their borrowers' (ADB 2000b: 44). Indeed, even where banks are represented on boards, it has been found that this is associated with easier finance, not more stringent monitoring.

Creditors also have the ability to play a large part in the governance system because of the control—through finance—they have on corporations. However, creditors themselves are corporations. In the case of Asia, many such creditors are as susceptible to governance faults as their debtors. In most cases the governance weaknesses of creditors limits their ability to influence the governance of their debtors. Thus, banks are not governed well either and have limited monitoring capacity.

The ADB survey of Thailand and Indonesia indicated that 'creditors have little or no influence over management decisions and, in cases where they do, the influence is exercised mainly through loan covenants' (ADB 2000b: 41). Relationships affect participation because they are used as collateral. Trust is an important feature. The reciprocal nature of this trust resulted in the lack of monitoring by banks. Greenspan (1999: 4) suggests that such financial infrastructure reform is needed to 'facilitate the trading of claims on businesses in open markets . . . rather than idiosyncratic bank loans'.

While post-crisis lending requirements have become more stringent, this does not translate into increased monitoring ability or influence on management decision-

---

9 The banking system was also culpable in allowing the existence of relationship-based finance to perpetuate. Banking sector reform will not be considered further except to the extent that banks themselves are corporations where similar corporate-style reforms are needed.

making. From a nominal economic perspective, to move to an arm's-length approach to transactions would inhibit access to capital (Skeel 1999: 27). Thus, corporations are unwilling to do so. Realistically, resistance arises because moving to an objective commercial lending environment prevents the maintenance of control. Relationships are important. The concept of stakeholder involvement itself is based on relationships. To alter current relationships, therefore, to resemble more professional commercial interaction and allow stakeholder participation, is an opportunity to influence good governance for the benefit of all investors.

Proposition four: the prevalence of insiders in current governance systems will affect compliance with increased disclosure and transparency regulations—OECD Principle IV.

It was established above that the influence of insiders stemmed from ownership structure and the role of relationships. It was also established that, regardless of which governance model, expropriation of wealth by corporate insiders—as a manifestation of the agency problem—was the greatest threat to good governance (La Porta *et al.* 2000a: 26). Here, the issue concerns the employment of measures preventing the exposure of insider misconduct, in particular, where control allows the preservation of information asymmetry.

Insiders form a closely held group that generally comprises founding members and entities with a close commercial association with the corporation. There are relatively loose financial controls within an insider system with relationships forming the essential control. Within this relationship-based transaction environment the need for disclosure and transparency is not crucial. In the annotated OECD Principles the statement is made that 'a strong disclosure regime can help attract capital and maintain confidence in the capital markets' (OECD 1999: 19). It explains the crucial monitoring role of disclosure and transparency in well-developed equity markets. The statement alludes to many of the benefits of disclosure to the establishment of a capital market directly pertinent to Asian post-crisis reform. However, current systems prevent disclosure and transparency in the current environment. Khanna and Palepu (1999) see transparency improving the investment in those emerging markets characterised by concentrated ownership. Again, ownership structure plays a crucial role in the implementation of the new Principles.

Transparency has been identified as a key requirement or feature of good governance. As with all governance mechanisms, the ultimate purpose of transparency is investor protection. Improved standards of disclosure create transparency and hence knowledge. The ability to protect oneself from harm is knowledge that others are in fact doing wrong. Primarily, knowledge increases investor protection as it corrects information asymmetry. In what may seem a simple observation, disclosure creates knowledge. Indeed, 'disclosure can be a powerful tool for influencing the behaviour of companies and for protecting investors' (OECD 1999: 19). It forces exposure and creates transparency.

However, Asia does not have a tradition of strong disclosure. Part of this tradition emanates from the control insiders have over systems. Factions within firms were able to dictate the type of information released, and to some extent this ability will always remain. Often this led to non-disclosure and opacity in corporate dealings. Deficiency in pre-crisis standards of transparency and accountability allowed corporate management to avoid disclosure of corporate activity, often through the suppression of information or systematic misinformation regarding impropriety and management practices. Now, disclosure and transparency are seen as imperative to achieving corporate accountability: that is, to make managers answerable for their behaviour.

Proposition five: contextual change will assist in the implementation of improved, but not global, standards.

While the OECD Principles set out specific guidelines that act as a benchmark against which compliance can be measured, a country should be scored against country-specific scorecards (despite the benefits of international standards). The problem with the use of Western standards, as Antons suggests, is that 'the question whether there is improvement or not is judged according to Western standards' (Antons 1995: 1). It is not an appropriate standard. Even when regional standards are chosen, difficulties remain.

Implementing advanced systems in developing countries may prove less effective than country-specific systems. The argument reflects the varying levels of national development around the world. Differences in stages of development will affect implementation For instance, the Commonwealth Association for Corporate Governance recognised that a 'universal code [is] not only inappropriate but undesirable' (CACG 1999: i). Thus the adoption of governance principles will be an adaptive process. Much like the formation of general principles, corporations will select a mixture of practices from the general pool to form their own body of governance. It should be recognised that the results of this process will not be less effective than the adoption of one particular code in full. The effectiveness and rate of change may be improved if governance is detailed to suit the particular circumstances of the corporate: the closely held firm. Family-controlled corporations will undoubtedly survive in the future. Thus, the issues relating to this form of corporation should be addressed.

It has been assumed that the OECD Principles were better, as a whole, than the systems that currently exist in Asia. However, the question must be asked whether in fact the existing systems were inherently unsuitable. Comparisons investigating whether one system is superior are difficult. It can be concluded that the models are different means to the same ends; existing relationship-based governance systems can still be effective. Schmidt and Spindler (1998) use the concept of complementarity to 'demonstrate that national corporate governance systems are usefully regarded as—possibly consistent—systems of complementary elements'. Similarly, Shleifer and Vishy (1997) do not see the need to replace one model of governance with another because (based on their extensive survey) they see all models as being complementary. Also, La Porta et al. (2000a) found that the less protective legal systems were complemented by other devices such as increased dividends. Finding which model is superior is not important, as long as it works for the circumstance. Importantly, Western governance is not necessarily categorically better and vice versa. Survival does not necessarily mean that a system is best, but that an alternative has been unable to develop.

There is a widely held conviction that the effectiveness of investor protection depends on the extent to which protection laws are enforced, or are enforceable. Table 3 provides information on the quality of Asian law and enforcement. The rule of law indicator is drawn from a collection of factors and is used here as evidence of enforcement capacity. From a possible score of 10, it is evident from Table 3 that the Asian crisis economies have an average of barely 5 across the three variables. Notably, Malaysia appears to provide better overall protection than the others, while Indonesia provides the worst.

Singling out corruption, it can be said that Asian enforcement agencies and legal institutions are vulnerable to claims of inherent corruption, shown by the figures in Table 3. Corruption can be defined as the misuse of office for personal gain. Inappropriate behaviour by members of legal institutions assists in explaining the lack of propensity to enforce. The issue of corruption provides an interesting reflection of the complex situation in Asia. The conclusion that can be drawn from Table 3 is most pertinent. Berkowitz et al. demonstrate that 'legal effectiveness . . . is not merely a function of the characteristics of formal law, but is also a function of various potential

Country	Judicial efficiency	Risk of law	Corruption
Indonesia	2.50	3.98	2.15
Republic of Korea	6.00	5.35	5.30
Malaysia	9.00	6.78	7.38
Philippines	4.75	2.73	2.92
Thailand	3.25	6.25	5.18

Table 3 RULE OF LAW INDICATORS IN ASIAN CRISIS ECONOMIES (SCORES OUT OF 10)

Source: La Porta *et al.* 1998

inefficiencies of implementation when law is transplanted into an "alien" implementing or enforcing environment' (Schauer 2000: 5). The inefficiency in this case lies in enforcement. Summarising the situation, the ADB declares, 'the basic regulatory structure . . . appears to be in place . . . poor compliance and enforcement appear to be the major problems' (ADB 2000b: 3). Wong (2000) goes further to suggest that weak enforcement had 'first-order' importance in determining the extent of the Asian Economic Crisis. The conclusion, therefore, is the clear need for improvement in enforcement so that, when improved governance standards are implemented, they will be effective. It is beyond the scope of this paper to discuss means for improving enforcement. Suffice to mention that obvious methods include the strengthening of regulatory powers of enforcement agencies, reducing corruption and increasing penalties for opportunistic behaviour. Reducing the opportunity with the development of sound enforcement mechanisms should effectively force good governance by reducing the ability to avoid it.

Given limited resources, a short-term choice between law and enforcement must be made. Arguably, many countries currently have adequate laws. Thus, priority should be given to enforcement over additional legal reform, particularly given the fact that laws—however ineffective—are basically useless if they are seldom enforced. The short-term balance is likely to provide greater benefits in the future as, once a strict enforcement regime is in place, it may become easier to enact new laws. Ultimately it is hoped that the law and its enforcement will both be equally effective.

Culture perpetuates through people. Thus, people are the main impediment to change. Implementing the Principles is dependent on people because 'at the end of the day you deal with individual institutions and you deal with individuals' (IMF 1999: 4). The ADB sees that 'people are the heart of development . . . [and] . . . are not only the ultimate beneficiaries of development, but are also the agents of development' (ADB 1995: 5). Likewise, cultural legacies will affect the reform decisions of governments. In tandem with change in the law, attempts must be made to change the attitudes of people to governance-related issues. To achieve the aim of establishing good corporate governance regimes, there is a need for an inherent culture of integrity, notably absent in Asia. The difficulty in changing culture is that people have been raised in a culture 'programmed' to work comfortably in it and thus will resist change. Hart (1995) sees Cadbury's approach of trying to educate companies, to facilitate an understanding of the value and principle of change, to persuade them to make changes in corporate governance as probably the best method. In time, resistance to change will be overcome by the costs of remaining stagnant.

The comment that the 'effectiveness of corporate governance systems cannot merely be legislated by law' (Confederation of Indian Industry 1998: 22) is appropriate when we consider that implementation is affected by people more so than by any other factor.

The report notes: 'the best results would be achieved when the companies begin to treat the code not as a mere structure, but as a way of life' (Confederation of Indian Industry 1998: 5). Equally, as the World Bank emphasises, governance initiatives win most support when driven from the bottom up rather than from the top down (World Bank Group 1999: 17). By its own admission, the World Bank has conceded that such development of necessary institutions and human capacity will 'take years'.

Conclusions

In retrospect, it is clear that the high-growth outcomes of many developing Asian economies concealed the absence of mechanisms necessary to control their developing economies, their financial sectors and corporations. Notably, inadequate control mechanisms impeded the detection of corporate misconduct. Corporate governance has been posited as redressing internal corporate failure by ensuring efficient and effective corporate management. The objective is to make Asian corporations an attractive investment to reclaim foreign capital and to encourage the high levels of domestic savings to remain in Asia. To do so requires addressing investor concerns regarding poor corporate control. Indeed, 'higher standards of corporate governance have been proposed as a means of increasing the accountability of users of funds to suppliers of funds' (Carson 1996: 3). The objective for governance reform is to inspire investor confidence by increasing the protection provided under governance.

Maturing corporate governance systems in Asia are ultimately likely to develop to address their own national, legal and business customs. The purported importance of corporate governance, however, can be seen as requiring expedience in reform. To this end, the adoption of internationally recognised standards of good governance has been posited as an appropriate and expedient method of reforming perceived problems and offers enterprises the chance to gain a share of future investment capital. Using the benchmark provides the capacity to develop domestic institutions quicker than would otherwise be possible through self-design—the quicker the better. The adoption of the OECD Principles is a small step in this direction.

This discussion has focused on the obstacles associated with attempting to expediently achieve improved corporate governance via the implementation of the OECD Principles. The objective was to establish if the ability to implement the Principles was negatively affected by culture. The results support the proposition that various cultural factors negatively affect the ability to implement the OECD Principles. Notably, the results illustrate that ownership structure (composition and concentration) has the most influence on implementation, and is related to the other factors investigated: the existence of insiders and the role of relationships. These conclusions are important because they reaffirmed areas of difficulty and hopefully highlighted areas that policy-makers may wish to concentrate on when correcting Asian corporate governance systems.

The challenges that confront this process are substantial and will differ for each country in the Asia–Pacific region. Therefore, complete and immediate convergence towards the OECD Principles is not possible in the short term. While no one model can accommodate such diversity, given a cultural shift—in the philosophical (relationships) and economic (finance) bases of the firm—contextual change methods suggest that effective governance systems might be implemented over the long term. Participation of people willing to work towards real corporate change is needed. For example, when reflecting on recent South Korean reform, President Kim Dae-jung (1999) drew one important conclusion: 'introducing new laws and institutions alone is not enough. Reform can succeed only when these institutional changes are accompanied by changes in people's attitude. This is the real test.'

References

ADB (Asian Development Bank) (1995) 'Governance: Sound Development Management', *Asian Development Bank Online Publication*, www.adb.org/documents/policies/governance/gov000.asp, August 1995.

ADB (Asian Development Bank) (1999) *Governance in Asia: From Crisis to Opportunity* (ADB Annual Report; Manila: ADB).

ADB (Asian Development Bank) (2000a) 'A Consolidated Report on Corporate Governance and Financing in East Asia: Executive Summary', *OECD Second Asian Roundtable on Corporate Governance*, Hong Kong, China, 31 May–2 June 2000 (Manila: ADB).

ADB (Asian Development Bank) (2000b) *Corporate Governance and Finance in East Asia: A Study of Indonesia, Republic of Korea, Malaysia, Philippines, and Thailand* (Vol. I, a consolidated report; Manila: ADB).

Allen, F. (2000) *Financial Structure and Financial Crisis* (Asian Development Bank Institute Working Paper Series, 10; Manila: Asian Development Bank, June 2000).

Alston, P. (1999) 'Transplanting Foreign Norms: Human Rights and Other International Legal Norms in Japan', *European Journal of International Law* 10.3: 625-32.

Antons, C. (1995) 'Analysing Asian Law: The Need for a General Concept', *Law in Context* 13.1 (Annual): 106-23.

Arceo-Dumlao, T. (2000a) 'Corporate Governance: A "Political Decision" ', *Philippine Daily Inquirer*, 20 June 2000.

Arceo-Dumlao, T. (2000b) 'Philippines: Growth with Equity. The Remaining Agenda', *Philippine Daily Inquirer*, 19 June 2000.

Asian Corporate Governance Association (2000) *Building Stronger Boards and Companies in Asia: A Concise Report on Corporate Governance Policies and Practices* (Asian Corporate Governance Association, January 2000).

Batten, J., and Y.H. Kim (2000) 'Expanding Long-Term Financing Through Bond Market Development: A Postcrisis Policy Task', *Asian Development Bank Conference on Government Bond Markets and Financial Sector Development in Developing Asian Economies*, 28–30 March, ADB Auditorium, Manila (Manila: Asian Development Bank).

Bebchuk, L.A., and M.J. Roe (1999) 'A Theory of Path Dependence in Corporate Ownership and Governance', *Stanford Law Review* 52: 127-69.

Berglof, E., and E.L. von Thadden (1999) 'The Changing Corporate Governance Paradigm: Implications for Transition and Developing Countries', *Annual Bank Conference on Development Economics*, 28–30 April 1999 (Washington, DC: World Bank): 135-62.

Berle, A., and G. Means (1932) *The Modern Corporation and Private Property* (New York: Macmillan).

CACG (Commonwealth Association for Corporate Governance) (1999) *CACG Guidelines, Principles for Corporate Governance in the Commonwealth: Towards Global Competitiveness and Economic Accountability* (Marlborough, New Zealand: CACG, http://combinet.net/Governance/FinalVer/finlvndx.htm).

Carson, E. (1996) 'Corporate Governance Disclosure in Australia: The State of Play', *Australian Accounting Review* 6.2: 3-10.

Claessens, S., S. Djankov, J.P.H. Fan and L.H.P. Lang (1999) *Corporate Diversification in East Asia: The Role of Ultimate Ownership and Group Affiliation* (World Bank Working Paper, 2089; Washington, DC: World Bank).

Claessens, S., S. Djankov and L.H.P. Lang (2000) 'The Separation of Ownership and Control in East Asian Corporations', *Journal of Financial Economics* 58.1–2: 81-112.

Coase, R. (1937) 'The Nature of the Firm', *Economica* 4 (November 1937): 386-405.

Confederation of Indian Industry (1998) *The Draft Report of the Committee on Corporate Governance* (Kumar Mangalam Committee, appointed by the SEBI on Corporate Governance; New Delhi: Confederation of Indian Industry).

Dyck, I.J.A. (2000) 'Ownership Structure, Legal Protections and Corporate Governance', *Annual Bank Conference on Development Economics*, 28–30 April 1999 (Washington, DC: World Bank).

Gilson, R.J. (2000) *Globalizing Corporate Governance: Convergence of Form or Function* (John M. Olin Program in Law and Economics, Working Paper, 192; Stanford, CA: Stanford Law School, May 2000).

Greenspan, A. (1999) 'Lessons from the Global Crisis', *The Federal Reserve Board* (The World Bank Group and the International Monetary Fund, Program of Seminars, Washington, DC, 27 September 1999; Washington, DC: World Bank).

Hart, O. (1995) 'Corporate Governance: Some Theory and Implications', *The Economic Journal* 105.430: 678-89.

Heuer, M., J.L. Cummings and W. Hutabarat (1999) 'Cultural Stability or Change among Managers in Indonesia', *Journal of International Business Studies* 30.3: 599-610.

Hopt, K., H. Kanda, M.J. Roe, E. Wymeersch and S. Prigge (1998) *Comparative Corporate Governance* (Oxford, UK: Clarendon Press).

IMF (International Monetary Fund) (1999) 'Report on Financial Sector Crisis and Restructuring: Lessons from Asia' (Press Briefing, 25 September 1999).

Jensen, M., and W. Meckling (1976) 'Theory of the Firm: Managerial Behaviour, Agency Costs and Ownership Structure', *Journal of Financial Economics* 3: 305-60.

Johnson, S., P. Boone, A. Breach and E. Friedman (2000) 'Corporate Governance in the Asian Financial Crisis', *Journal of Financial Economics* 58.1–2: 141-86.

Jordan, C. (1999) 'Corporate Governance in Asia and the Asian Financial Crisis: Evidence of the Impact and Current Trends', *OECD and Korea Development Institute Conference, Corporate Governance in Asia: A Comparative Perspective*, Seoul, 3–5 March 1999 (Paris: Organisation for Economic Co-operation and Development).

Khanna, T., and K. Palepu (1999) 'The Right Way to Restructure Conglomerates in Emerging Markets', *Harvard Business Review*, July/August 1999.

Kim, D.J. (1999) 'Opening Address', *Korean Government and World Bank Conference, Democracy, Market Economy and Development*, Seoul, 26–27 February 1999 (Manila: Asian Development Bank).

Krugman, P. (1998) 'What Happened to Asia?', mimeo, www.hartford-hwp.com/archives/50/010.html, 16 January 1998.

La Porta, R., F. Lopez-De-Silanes, A. Shleifer and R. Vishy (1998) 'Law and Finance', *Journal of Political Economy* 106.6: 1113-55.

La Porta, R., F. Lopez-De-Silanes, A. Shleifer and R. Vishy (2000a) 'Agency Problems and Dividend Policies around the World', *Journal of Finance* 55.1: 1-34.

La Porta, R., F. Lopez-De-Silanes, A. Shleifer and R. Vishy (2000b) 'Investor Protection and Corporate Governance', *Journal of Financial Economics* 58.1-2: 3-27.

Nam, I.C., Y. Kang and J.K. Kim (1999) 'Comparative Corporate Governance Trends in Asia', *OECD and Korea Development Institute Conference, Corporate Governance in Asia: A Comparative Perspective*, Seoul, 3–5 March 1999 (Paris: Organisation for Economic Co-operation and Development).

Nestor, S., and J. Thompson (1999) 'Corporate Governance Patterns in OECD Economies: Is convergence under way?', *OECD and Korea Development Institute Conference, Corporate Governance in Asia: A Comparative Perspective*, Seoul, 3–5 March 1999 (Paris: Organisation for Economic Co-operation and Development).

OECD (Organisation for Economic Co-operation and Development) (1999) *Principles of Corporate Governance* (Paris: OECD).

Rubach, M.J., and T.C. Sebora (1998) 'Comparative Corporate Governance: Competitive Implications of an Emerging Convergence', *Journal of World Business* 33.2 (Summer 1998): 167-84.

Schauer, F. (2000) *The Politics and Incentives of Legal Transplantation* (Center for International Development Working Paper, 44; Cambridge, MA: Harvard University, April 2000).

Schmidt, R.H., and G. Spindler (1998) *Path Dependence, Corporate Governance and Complementarity: A Comment on Bebchuk and Roe* (Working Paper Series: Finance and Accounting; Frankfurt am Main: Goethe University, December 1998).

Shleifer, A., and R.W. Vishy (1997) 'A Survey of Corporate Governance', *Journal of Finance* 52.2: 737-83.

Skeel, D.A. (1999) 'An Evolutionary Theory of Corporate Law and Corporate Bankruptcy', *Corporate Practice Commentator* 41.1.

Wong, K.K. (2000) 'Corporate Governance and the Asian Financial Crisis', *Malaysian Business*, Kuala Lumpur, 1 June 2000.

World Bank Group (1997) 'Cadbury leaves a bitter taste for smaller companies', *Management Today*, April 1997.

World Bank Group (1999) *Corporate Governance: A Framework for Implementation (Overview)* (Washington, DC: World Bank Group).

Discovering the Needle of Trust in the Haystack of Distrust

International and Corporate Citizenship Alliances: Indian/Australian Experiences

David Kimber

School of Management, RMIT Business, Australia

S. Raghunath

Indian Institute of Management Bangalore, India

Trust is a key aspect in the development of business relationships. Considerable research on trust is taking place in psychological, organisational and sociological fields of study. This paper summarises recent research findings and reviews a study of trust in international alliances (IA). Four joint venture case studies were investigated by interviewing IA managers in India and Australia. Findings confirmed the significance of trust and correlate a number of the issues identified in previous trust theory. A number of other issues were identified that influence IA and corporate citizenship maintenance. The paper proposes that the importance of trust is also dependent on the nature of the industry, the type of joint venture project and the socioeconomic and legal/control environment. The paper confirms that trust is a multidimensional, dynamic factor which is important for the development of IA or corporate–community relationships.

- Corporate citizenship
- Strategic alliances
- Trust theory
- Relationships
- International joint ventures
- Ethics and values

David Kimber is currently an Associate Professor in the School of Management at RMIT and has been Project Director for the St James Ethics Centre, Melbourne Office. He was the former Associate Dean and Director of Post Graduate Studies at the Faculty of Business, RMIT, Melbourne, Australia. He is on the interim board of the Australian Corporate Citizenship Alliance. David is the research co-ordinator for the Business Integrity Systems Analysis research project supported by Transparency International, Arthur Andersen, Telstra and BHP.

✉ School of Management, RMIT Business, 239 Bourke St, Melbourne, Australia 3000

🖥 davidk@rmit.edu.au

🌐 www.bf.rmit.edu.au

S. Raghunath is Professor of Corporate Strategy and Policy at Indian Institute of Management Bangalore, India. He was a visiting scholar at the Graduate School of Business, Stanford University, USA. He is on the board of the Strategic Management Forum of India, and the Society of Certified Investment Bankers of India. His research interests include strategic leadership in strategic networks, business alliances and joint ventures and e-business transformation. He has published several papers and case studies. His consulting work has focused on how business leaders can create value for customers in a hyper-competitive market and on issues relating to development of cohesive organisations to champion and sustain growth.

✉ Indian Institute of Management Bangalore, Bannerghatta Road, Bangalore, India 560 076

🖥 srnath@iimb.ernet.in

🌐 www.iimb.ernet.in

W

HY DO FIRMS GET INTO AN ALLIANCE? ONE ASPECT IS TO ADDRESS opportunity efficiently and effectively in the world of economic opportunism. When economic opportunism is the goal, how does one ensure that the same intent does not vitiate the joint contribution of capabilities to mine the pot of gold buried in the existing and emerging markets? When potential partners get together, they experience each other through the smokescreen of preliminary knowledge, untested assumptions and prior experience, both relevant and irrelevant to alliance management. It is as if they are searching for the needle of trust in the haystack of distrust, a haystack that has self-generating properties, a haystack full of wild weeds possessing self-propagating genes to withstand annihilation. Partners to an alliance directly and indirectly attempt to burn, destroy, eliminate distrust. This paper presents evidence of distrust reduction behaviour in Indian and Australian alliances and highlights the importance of context in trust-enhancing, distrust-reducing mechanisms.

Alongside this economic opportunism argument flows a growing sequence of literature which suggests that many in the world are becoming increasingly alarmed at the impact of corporations who take little account of their goals in anything other than economic or financial terms (Hutton 1995; Ralston Saul 1997). Corporate sustainability is becoming increasingly linked to social and environmental sustainability. A movement built around the concepts of corporate citizenship and corporate social responsibility is growing. Corporations are facing increasing pressures to work in co-operation with social groups, not-for-profit entities, government agencies, etc. to ensure that healthy societies underpin a healthy economy.

Consequently, a study of the key factors that affect the ability of partners to pursue their opportunism together directly, or to work in society as effective corporate citizens, relates to their ability to manage their trust or distrust towards their partners and stakeholders.

The dominant purposes of alliance formation can be seen from two perspectives. First, their purpose can be to access and utilise the complementary resources of partnering firms to strengthen existing products and services in existing markets or in new markets, or develop new products and services for existing or new markets. The leading perspective is the resource-based view, which was developed from the work of Penrose (1959) and advanced, for example, by Wernerfelt (1984), Corner (1991), Barney (1991), Collis and Montgomery (1995) and Pankaj Ghemawat (1999). In order to reduce time to market, achieve top-line and bottom-line targets and beat competition, firms search for alternatives. In the process of this search, firms find alliances to be appropriate vehicles for the utilisation of complementary capabilities.

Transaction cost economics, developed mainly by Williamson (1975, 1985), explains relational risk due to opportunism and dependence as a result of specific investment. Relational risk has two broad dimensions: the extent of loss one may incur due to opportunistic behaviour of the partner and the probability that this loss will occur. The extent of loss depends on the value of the partner in comparison to the next best opportunity, plus the switching cost to that alternative, which together determine one's dependence.

The probability that this loss will occur depends on the incentives the partner has for opportunistic behaviour and trustworthiness, explained by Nooteboom (1999) as 'propensity towards opportunism', which in turn depends on character, bonding between partners, habits and institutions.

Second, alliances may be formed as a protective strategy to minimise the risk of factors other than economic opportunism limiting organisations' capacity to grow or survive. Multinational corporations (MNCs) in particular are being forced to protect their reputations in an increasingly hostile social environment (Balasubrumanian and Kimber 2000).[1] One way in which organisations are attempting to deal with this trend is to form

---

1 The risk of not doing so in many circumstances has proved to be detrimental to corporate reputa-

alliances and relationships with stakeholder representatives, either groups or individuals, to work out mutually acceptable solutions. 'Unholy alliances' such as mining corporations and indigenous communities, oil producers and environmental activist non-governmental organisations (NGOs) are becoming more common. The creation of business and community partnerships is becoming a global movement.

Consequently, trust is a topic moving into centre stage as a key management issue. Likewise 'international alliances' and 'relationship-building' are playing increasingly important roles in the globalisation of business. This paper reviews the connection between these two areas. First, it defines the terms and sets out a conceptual framework for the discussion. American research on trust in the last ten years is briefly outlined and a study of the application of trust in international joint ventures (IJVs) in India and Australia is reviewed. Findings from that study are presented and correlated with the research. The paper concludes by identifying aspects of trust theory that have been confirmed by the study and highlights practical issues that relate specifically to trust, relationship-building and IJVs.

While the research focus of the paper relates to IJVs, it is posited that new forms of alliance, especially those emerging from corporate citizenship developments, community–business partnerships, increased stakeholder involvement with corporations, etc., will be well advised to take account of trust research and theory. Recognition of this arena is likely to enhance greater interaction between corporations, community groups and society—a development that can only enhance the corporate citizenship movement.

The conceptual framework

Trust is not a new term. It is commonly used and has been a key influence on human behaviour for centuries. It has been the focus for many myths, legends and fables that deal with the way people and the gods have behaved. However, even though it is a key human value, trust has not been central to philosophical discourse (Baier 1992). She suggests that trust has connections with 'soft', emotional, subjectivity and, as such, has been discounted by many male philosophers who have reviewed moral, ethical behaviour in the light of conflict rather than harmony.

The advent of internationalisation, a greater emphasis on relationship-building rather than managing conflict, and a growing awareness of the importance of economic co-operation, have led to a re-evaluation of the importance of trust as a business issue in the last three decades. A body of research has been rapidly expanding in a variety of fields. Academics in politics, sociology, psychology, communications, economics and management or organisational behaviour have all taken up trust research. As indicated by a number of American literature reviews (McKnight and Chervany 1996; Sheppard and Sherman 1998; Rousseau *et al.* 1998), a wide variety of orientations have developed. McKnight and Chervany's extensive survey on the meanings of trust has provided an approach that assists in developing theory. They identified a wide range of trust meanings but conclude that 'a broad, cohesive yet parsimonious group of constructs emerges'. These are: trusting intention, trusting behaviour, trusting beliefs, system trust, dispositional trust and a situational decision to trust. This conceptual framework flows in sequence from attitudes and beliefs through intention and behaviour, disposition and systems to situational decision-making. Such an approach assists researchers in focusing on a specific trust arena and correlating their activities thematically with other research. This paper concentrates on beliefs, intention and behaviour.

---

tion. Cases relating to social or environmental disasters, such as the Union Carbide gas leak in Bhopal, the *Exxon Valdez* oil tanker shipwreck, Shell Oil's problems with politics in Nigeria and oil rig dismantling in the North Sea, illustrate this point.

The meaning of trust

A number of perspectives of trust emerge, which are directly relevant to IJVs. First, trusting beliefs suggest that a psychological condition (Rousseau *et al.* 1998) underpins trust. Without this 'state of mind', activity cannot progress. McKnight and Chervany suggest that trusting beliefs are built around a view that people are (can be) 'benevolent, honest, competent and predictable'. They suggest 'the combination of the four beliefs provides a firm foundation for trusting intention and trusting behaviour'.

A number of other elements are commonly associated with trust. The first theme identified by many researchers (Rousseau *et al.* 1998) relates to vulnerability (Mayer *et al.* 1995) with a concomitant belief that trust provides security (Lewis and Weigert 1985; Rempel *et al.* 1985; Eayrs 1993).

Risk is the second theme identified in the research literature. It is an 'essential condition in psychological, sociological and economic conceptions of trust' (Rousseau *et al.* 1998: 395). Risk must be known by the 'trustor', otherwise trust would not apply as a concept influencing behaviour or decision-making.

Interdependence (Rousseau *et al.* 1998) or dependence (Dobing 1993) is the third condition regularly identified in trust theory. Trust implies that a relationship exists between two parties, whereby either one relies on the other, or there is mutual reliance. IJVs are often based on the latter condition.

Rousseau *et al.* (1998) and Nooteboom *et al.* (1997) provide definitions of trust that summarise these themes as follows: 'Trust is a psychological state comprising the intention to accept vulnerability based upon the positive expectations of the intentions of another' (Rousseau *et al.* 1998: 395). 'Trust is a partner's ability to perform according to the intentions and expectations of a relationship (competence trust) or his/her intentions not to defect (intentional trust)' (Nooteboom *et al.* 1997: 311).

Other factors affecting trust

Research has identified a wide variety of other factors that impact on trust. At one end of a spectrum trust has been identified as relating to a static, single-item event. What causes a person to trust another when faced with a single decision (Axelrod 1984)?[2] Alternatively, and more commonly in organisational contexts, trust has been considered as a dynamic element in relationships which can be constructively developed and maintained, or can decline (Rousseau *et al.* 1998; Miles and Creed 1995).

An important, more recently identified view is that trust and mistrust can exist as independent variables in a relationship, rather than at either end of a spectrum (Lewicki *et al.* 1998). Lewicki *et al.* conclude that they operate simultaneously during a relationship and put forward the framework outlined in Table 1.

Their analysis suggests that the simultaneous existence of these two conditions is most likely in rapidly changing or unstable environments. This is particularly relevant for IJVs in new or emerging industries such as information technology. Two entities may implicitly trust each other's technical expertise and rely on each other's involvement supporting the JV accordingly. However, as has been recognised in JV research (Raghunath 1996a, 1998b), each party may be aware of the other's potential to become a future competitor in the market and, therefore, they 'mistrust' each other in terms of market information. As such, it is not uncommon for parties involved in such an IJV to erect 'paper walls' around the IJV to protect themselves. The parties may be quite mistrustful of each other in terms of future market development strategies. However, they are

---

2 Axelrod's 'Prisoner's Dilemma' research is typical of this sort of analysis

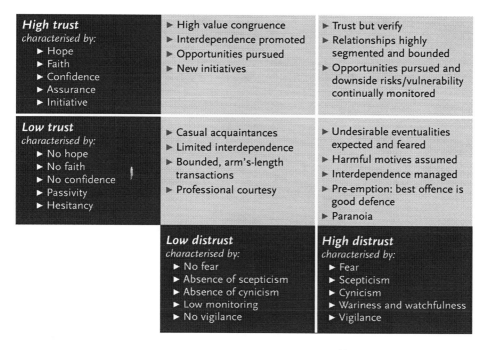

High trust *characterised by:* ▶ Hope ▶ Faith ▶ Confidence ▶ Assurance ▶ Initiative	▶ High value congruence ▶ Interdependence promoted ▶ Opportunities pursued ▶ New initiatives	▶ Trust but verify ▶ Relationships highly segmented and bounded ▶ Opportunities pursued and downside risks/vulnerability continually monitored
Low trust *characterised by:* ▶ No hope ▶ No faith ▶ No confidence ▶ Passivity ▶ Hesitancy	▶ Casual acquaintances ▶ Limited interdependence ▶ Bounded, arm's-length transactions ▶ Professional courtesy	▶ Undesirable eventualities expected and feared ▶ Harmful motives assumed ▶ Interdependence managed ▶ Pre-emption: best offence is good defence ▶ Paranoia
	Low distrust *characterised by:* ▶ No fear ▶ Absence of scepticism ▶ Absence of cynicism ▶ Low monitoring ▶ No vigilance	**High distrust** *characterised by:* ▶ Fear ▶ Scepticism ▶ Cynicism ▶ Wariness and watchfulness ▶ Vigilance

Table 1 TRUST–DISTRUST MATRIX
Source: Lewicki *et al.* 1998: 445

prepared to work together and trust each other to gain mutual technological advantage via an IJV.[3]

Trust has been identified as both a 'cause' and 'effect' in terms of relationship development. It has been described as a key element determining how relationships are built and maintained (Deutsch 1958; Williamson 1975). It has also been regularly noted as an outcome of good relationships: namely, trust builds trust (Mishra 1996; Rousseau *et al.* 1998).

Schemas of trust have been identified in a number of ways. Research that comes from economic analysis considers trust as a calculative event, predictable and based on rational choice. People or entities will trust each other based on knowledge of proven prior performance, evaluation based on certification, reputation, history of past performance, rational choice, economic exchange assessment, etc. In contrast, the sociological/psychological perspective recognises relational issues. Then trust is perceived as an interpersonal, 'affective', emotionally influenced interaction between people either individually or in groups (McAllister 1995). Such an approach emphasises the intuitive, subjective feelings that people have about each other. Trust emerges from the relationship itself; personal factors will have significant impact.

Another schema of trust suggests that it has meaning as a concept at four levels (Miles and Creed 1965; Fukuyama 1995; Rousseau *et al.* 1998; Whitener *et al.* 1998):

▶ Interpersonal (one-to-one relationships)[4]

▶ Group/organisational (relationships between groups in formally structured environments such as at work)

---

3 Lewicki *et al.* describe such a JV which existed between Boeing Corporation and a Japanese company involved in the building of the Boeing 777.

▶ Small group/community (relationships between groups in informally structured environments such as neighbourhoods and social clubs)

▶ Large group/institutional/societal (relationships between individuals and groups at institutional/societal levels; in schools, relating to law and order, etc.)[5]

These two frameworks can be combined to reflect the potential, multi-channelled, multi-faceted set of relationships that co-exist and influence each other simultaneously.

The 'X' in Table 2 represents the hypothetical likelihood of the different styles having a different emphasis at different levels (more Xs = higher probability). This model suggests that calculative trust will be more evident when considering trust at societal or institutional level, and that relational trust between individuals is likely to have little or no impact, while at the interpersonal level relational trust styles are likely to be more influential.

Trust levels	Trust styles			
	Primarily calculative ⟵⟶			*Primarily relational*
Interpersonal	XX	XXX	XXXX	XXXXX
Group/organisational	XXXX	XXX	XXX	XX
Group/community	XX	XXX	XXXX	XXX
Large group/institutional/societal	XXX	X		

Table 2 TRUST LEVELS AND STYLES

Such a matrix highlights a key trust issue. People relate to each other at all levels, and are likely to use different styles of trusting behaviour and beliefs in different circumstances. They may trust a professional or tradesperson very much on a calculative basis while responding to friends and work colleagues in a more relational way. At the same time they might be members of groups that exhibit both high and low trust reactions to other groups or individuals in different settings. The matrix emphasises the point that trust as a concept rarely exists in isolation and is highly contextual. It highlights that, in corporate–community partnership development, both calculative and relational trust factors are likely to be influential.

This approach can be extended to reflect the impact of national culture on trust practices (Doney *et al.* 1998). Doney *et al.*'s analysis suggests that different styles will be adopted in different cultural environments. They use Hofstede's dimensions of culture (Hofstede 1980) as the basis for a series of hypotheses that indicate how different countries' cultural styles are likely to encourage different types of trust behaviour. Hagen's (1998) analysis of trust in Japan suggests that situational factors, such as the importance of trade group relationships in Japan, influence the potential for the betrayal of trust.

Das and Teng (1998) review the relationship between trust and control mechanisms used to manage distrust. They present a number of hypotheses that relate trust and control levels to different types of alliance. They suggest that high trust and good control

---

4 Another area of trust relates to the 'individual', i.e. trusting oneself. It emerges from psychological themes of self-deception, self-confidence, self-doubt, etc. and is worthy of consideration, but is outside the boundaries of this paper.
5 At this level it is the trust behaviour of a critical mass—the larger social groups such as religious communities and societies—and is influenced by both culture and structural support systems.

systems will help to create joint ventures. When trust levels are low and control systems are hard to establish, non-equity alliances are most appropriate. Minority-party equity alliances will emerge when there is low trust and good control systems or vice versa.

The relationships between risk and interdependence and relational forms have been analysed by a number of researchers and are summarised by Sheppard and Sherman (1998). They have developed a model that helps to clarify potential relationships and behaviours. Their extension of the concepts of different types and levels of trust are outlined in Table 3.

To conclude the review of the different aspects of trust research, it can be suggested that balance and consistency are likely to be temporary states in many situations. Equilibrium is often a snapshot of a moving continuum of interaction influencing and influenced by trust and distrust simultaneously. This becomes increasingly relevant to a global world influenced by dynamic and rapidly changing organisations that want to use joint venturing as an approach to expansion and market development. Similarly, MNCs being pressured to take account of a wider group of stakeholders need to take account of trust research. It would suggest that interpersonal trust may have more applicability when calculative or institutional trust becomes more problematic. However, rapidly changing environments are likely to break the connections that help build up relational trust. The effect of downsizing and restructuring on the personal relationships may be an important factor that should be taken into account in the development of a new IJV. In the merger and acquisition climate, this key factor may be overlooked in the swirl of global decision-making in MNCs. Consequently, trust management and its impact on the development of IJVs in Australia and India in the last five years is an important field worthy of further research.

Indian and Australian cases studies: methodology

In 1997 and 1998 a series of interviews were carried out with four organisations directly involved with joint venturing. Two IJVs were chosen in India. Both were set up as

Table 3 TRUST RELATIONSHIPS AND BEHAVIOURS

Source: Sheppard and Sherman 1998: 431

Forms of dependence	Risks	Qualities of trustworthiness	Mechanism for trust	Relational mechanisms	Institutional mechanisms
Shallow dependence	Indiscretion Unreliability	Discretion Reliability Competence	Deterrence	Fate Control	Historical records Enforcement
Deep dependence	Cheating Abuse Neglect Self-esteem	Integrity Concern Benevolence	Obligation	Network	Quadratic control Socialisation Selection
Shallow interdependence	Poor co-ordination	Predictability Consistency	Discovery	Contiguity	Communication and information systems
Deep interdependence	Misanticipation	Foresight Intuition Empathy	Internalisation	Shared meaning, values, products, goals	Strategic alignment, common membership, discourse

independent entities from their parent companies. Both were involved in information technology development: one in the aircraft industry, the other in medical equipment research. In Australia interviews were conducted with personnel from the international divisions of two MNCs operating in the finance industry. The two Australian corporations were chosen because of recent significant offshore joint venturing activities. One had just won a licence to operate in mainland China, the other has been developing extensive networks in South and South-East Asia. A further interview was undertaken in Australia with an experienced independent consultant who has been working on IJV development for the past two decades, to verify the findings from the four cases.

The open-ended interviews were conducted using a series of questions to encourage discussion and trigger ideas relating to management. The questions covered the following themes:

▶ What does trust mean in terms of an IJV?

▶ Determination of its importance and techniques used to develop trust

▶ Clarification of conscious or unconscious processes used to deal with trust or mistrust issues emerging in IJV management

▶ How does timing and time management influence trust maintenance?

▶ Other strategic/policy management factors that have an impact on trust maintenance

The way the interviews were conducted emphasised 'focused informality'. In India they were conducted by both researchers working as a team; in Australia by one researcher. The interviews, in most cases, were tape-recorded and transcripts made to create initial data. The transcripts were initially analysed both independently by the researchers and then, later, as a team. The findings outlined below emerged from this analysis.

Research findings

Many of the findings correlated with the research outlined above. However, some modified the more extreme reflections that postulate that trust is the most significant element influencing the development of IJVs.

The importance of trust at the early stages of IJV negotiation

All parties interviewed strongly endorsed the view that trust is an essential factor at early stages of an IJV. Most parties identified approaches that helped to develop a trusting relationship. In one case 'distrust signposts' were specifically removed at the first meeting. For example, an attempt by a legal adviser to one partner in the project to have a confidentiality contract[6] signed before negotiation started was strongly resisted by senior negotiators from the other organisation. They regarded the need for such a document as a sign of distrust. It would start the relationship off on a negative footing. They indicated that, if it was seen as an essential aspect of the negotiations by the other party, the likelihood of the IJV succeeding was not high. This argument was accepted and the legal advice was ignored. In other cases, active steps were planned to include all key players in early deliberations. Workshops were used to ensure people affected by the project were kept informed of the proceedings, in order to reduce uncertainty. Such actions confirmed that trust underpins positive interaction between parties, is built via beliefs and attitudes, and is reinforced by behaviour.

The significance of relational trust

Personal intimacy was noted by a number of interviewees. The good personal relationships between the key people, often the senior decision-makers, was highlighted as a factor that helped to establish an IJV. Hand-written personal memos were noted as a way of developing personal connectedness by one CEO. In another case small gifts were given: stamps for the other partner's children, books on specific topics discussed, etc. Such actions showed an awareness of personal interests and were noted as gestures that helped to build relational trust.

An interesting note was that this issue was discussed by Indian IJV managers but not by the Australian international trade personnel. The Australian consultant said that he felt Australians were often insensitive to the more personal aspects of trust-building. They were not 'culturally prepared' and as such missed out on recognising the personal issues that helped to establish trust. Such findings correlate with research done on the preparation of Australian managers for international project work (Blackman 1994).

This result confirmed Macneil's (1980) view. He said: 'Relational exchange is based on a social component, largely represented by trust. Specifically, parties involved in relational exchange derive non-economic satisfactions and engage in social exchange as well as economic exchange' (Macneil 1980: 13).

This line of reasoning is consistent with the work of sociologists such as Powell (1990) and Granovetter (1985) who developed the notion of embeddedness. These scholars have emphasised the role played by socially embedded personal relationships in economic exchange. Economic exchange relations depart from 'pure economic motives' and 'become over laid with social content that carries strong expectations of trust and abstention from opportunism' (Granovetter 1985: 490).

Trust and distrust management as part of the total package of relationship-building

Most parties identified the need for a solid foundation for an IJV relationship. They indicated that it must be built on a sound awareness of all factors: social, economic, political, structural, operational systems, etc. As such, trust and mistrust management will influence how the relationship is developed. The Indian cases identified the need for 'paper walls' as noted above as part of mistrust management. Staff allegiance to the JV, rather than the international parents, was noted as an important organisational factor by one of the Indian cases. This was done by ensuring that the partner 'macro' decision-making was kept separate from the operational arena of the IJV. Both Indian cases created separate financial entities for the IJVs. In both of the Australian cases, the operational control systems were emphasised as important elements in a successful IJV. These features indicated the need to manage mistrust as well as to strengthen trust. Both these approaches confirmed the features of relationships that exist when high trust and distrust operate simultaneously, as noted in Table 1. Our research reinforces a view that high trust and high distrust is likely to be found in the IJV environment, especially when longer-term, technically complex relationships are implicit.

The development of trust takes time

It was evident in all cases that time is a crucial factor in the development of trust. In one of the Indian IJVs, the two parties had been trading or relating to each other for over 30

---

6 A contract that bound both parties not to divulge what would be discussed in the meeting to outside parties.

years. One of the Australian organisations obtained a licence to operate in another country after negotiating for over five years. They expected to be committed to the IJV for 20–30 years. Rapid trade development is often alluded to as a feature of globalisation. However, it is worth recognising the importance of time. It confirms that calculative trust is an important factor in larger organisational situations. Clarifying reputation and establishing an awareness of technical skills and capacity of the other partner is not likely to occur quickly and will be important if the relationship is to continue over a long period.

In essence we argue that inter-firm relationships develop with the context of recurring transactions between the parties. Social elements and relational norms epitomised by trust become established in the relationship (Ring and van de Ven 1992). The parties to the IJV rely on relational norms to adopt process elements that serve as safeguards in their relationship, contributing to a more durable, stable, long-term relationship.

Assessment of integrity

A corollary of the point identified above was the importance of integrity. All cases indicated that the development of trust and the strength of the relationship were directly influenced by the assessment of the partner's reliability, competence and credibility. As one of the Australian corporations noted, 'our prime concern is to establish a relationship with a quality partner'. Again, this directly relates to establishing trust in a 'calculative' way. The findings suggest that this will be more important when commitments to the IJV are high. Capital costs in developing infrastructure in another country are likely to be substantial. In certain areas, especially those influenced by government regulation such as the finance industry, a failed first venture could stop further opportunities for starting again with another partner.

Implications

A number of implications can be drawn from the research undertaken to date and the cases researched in India and Australia.

Confirmation of former research

The findings from this research project did not produce any contradictory findings to the prior research work on trust theory. It confirmed a number of key principles: namely, the ability of organisations to simultaneously manage trust and distrust, the importance of both relational and calculative trust and the significance of complexity and context, which is discussed in more detail below. The research also confirmed some of the factors that have an impact on trust creation and development previously identified.[7]

At the same time a simple model is proposed that combines some of the aspects of former research and draws on the findings from this project. It is outlined below.

Importance of context and complexity

Context is a significant factor which reduces the prospect for simple overall hypotheses to be drawn and proven when considering IJV development. This was illustrated by the cases and confirmed by discussions with the independent consultant. The industries considered highlighted two issues. The finance industry, especially with products such as insurance and long-term lending, create connections with customers that have to be handled for a long time. Consequently, international alliances (IAs) must be planned as a long-term operation. As such, systems must be established that can be sustained over a long period. An IJV in this field ideally must be between mature businesses: entities that will be able to co-exist over a long period. Here, calculative trust mechanisms and approaches will be most important. While relational trust may assist in the establishment of the IJV, ultimately in this industry trust-strengthening, mistrust-limiting financial control systems will be essential if the IJV is able to sustain market credibility.

In the technology industry environment, relational trust is more likely to be influential. Establishing control systems in areas undergoing rapid change is more difficult and possibly less manageable. Why establish an intricate financial control system if new products, changes in strategy, etc. are likely? In such environments, approaches that enhance and strengthen interpersonal trust may be more valuable. Relational trust-building approaches, such as encouraging and rewarding ethical conduct, may be more effective than concentrating on systems to manage distrust.

While the cases appear on the surface to provide some simple predictors in this arena, closer reflection suggests that simple solutions are unlikely. The dynamic and multi-faceted nature of trust and IJV development was confirmed in each case. Each case had certain individual features which meant drawing broadly based conclusions too strongly would be problematic.

Trust theory, networks and multiple alliances

In a world of rapid technology development and change, it can be posited that multiple alliances or networks are emerging as expansion or market share protection devices. Examples are most evident in the airlines and IT/communications industries.[8] They may relate to a specific technology development or may be used to keep 'a finger in a pie that is being continually rebaked'; a strategy to protect against being left behind during periods of rapid change. As such, these connections can be transitory, opportunistic, but still strategically significant.

This research emphasises the need to clearly identify the trust elements, or the appropriate distrust management systems needed to develop or maintain these entities. A loose R&D alliance to consider a specific technology application to be shared by all parties may be strongly influenced by the relational trust between the scientists involved. The control systems relating to seat allocation, booking and scheduling for an airlines alliance need to be foolproof, to ensure that overall market share of the group is expanded and no individual party's position is damaged.

Corporate citizenship alliances

Much of the paper so far has concentrated on IJVs as technical, market development-focused, primarily driven by the economic or financial imperative. However, the emerging importance of corporate reputation and citizenship is leading to MNCs forging relationships with other groups representing social and environment communities. Resources and energy corporations are being forced to refocus their strategies towards sustainability. Manufacturers are re-evaluating the impact of their production processes and products on the communities around them. Former 'radical' NGOs are increasingly been turned to by corporations concerned about their own lack of knowledge in community and environmental affairs.

7 A literature review undertaken in 1995 on trust in business indicated that key factors influencing trust were co-operation and sharing, time, good communication, appropriate behaviour, positivity, care, reliability and stability, equity and fairness. For further details, see Kimber and Birchall 1998.
8 Examples are Star Alliance, which linked a number of independent airlines, and TV and telecommunications networks such as those created by Star TV in India and China.

Understanding the implications of how trust is built or lost, especially with former 'enemies' who are now 'uncontrollable, often suspicious, allies', is an important dimension for the corporate citizenship movement. Relational trust is important, especially if interest groups are represented by strong personalities holding entrenched views. In Australia some mining companies' relationships with indigenous communities, whose land rights and cultural heritage have been threatened by mining, have become benchmark examples of corporate citizenship in action, primarily because the trust factor was appropriately managed.

Social and cultural awareness

As MNCs develop links in new and emerging economies, awareness of sociocultural factors becomes a more significant influence on their success. They have come to realise that their expatriate managers must be adept at gathering social and cultural understanding, and be able to adapt to local conditions, if they are to operate in a way that respects regional economies' needs and interests. Trust theory awareness will greatly enhance the chances of this occurring. Minimising behaviours that encourage distrust, and understanding how trust develops in the local context, will directly affect an MNC's ability to 'understand' how to operate effectively in that region. It is an issue that will influence the development of new IJVs, as well as relating existing stakeholders. It was a point strongly emphasised by the consultant commenting on the failure of MNCs attempting to work in China and is an oft-cited factor relating to the failure of MNCs' initial ventures in India.[9]

An alliance model of trust/distrust management

From our findings and reflecting on the implications, we have put forward a schema that may help us to understand how trust/distrust management will affect relationship-building. This schema is represented diagrammatically in Figure 1.We suggest that the phases of trust development are likely to be as follows:

Pre-relationship

Before the relationship, no trust or distrust between the parties will exist. If trust exists in any form, a relationship must have been established. Hence any new relationship exists either without trust, or with distrust assumed. This state must be a pre-existent condition before any relationship develops and can be regarded as the 'bedrock' on which the alliance will be built. It automatically establishes the need for trust-building behaviours to either overcome distrust or change the no-trust situation.

Preparing for a relationship

The initial, or ex-ante, phase of an alliance is likely to incorporate calculative trust establishment activity. This will aim either to overcome natural distrust or to establish a basis on which the relationship can develop. The activity is likely to be undertaken to establish the credibility of the potential partner(s). Reputation will be established by researching data or seeking opinions of others to establish prior performance. Parties

9 Enron's initial, expensive failure to establish an IJV for a power plant in India has been at least partially attributed to its inability to connect effectively with local communities, something it has now addressed (see Shrivastava and Venkateswaran 2000).

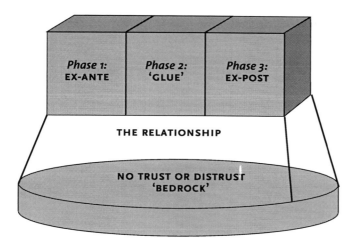

Figure 1 HOW TRUST/DISTRUST MANAGEMENT AFFECTS RELATIONSHIP-BUILDING

may use certification such as ISO registration standards, government registration (official corporation status, etc.) to attract potential 'suitors'. Relational trust, such as friendship between the key players, may initiate this phase but, in IJVs in particular, some calculative trust measures are likely to be important. In the exploratory phase of the IJV, trust is established through reputation. The companies and business leaders involved with those companies acquire reputations for probity and technical competence, which are known in the marketplace and among peers. Reputation as a basis for trust is seen to define the inherent attributes of the firm concerned. In this phase, trust is based on two key elements:

▶ Market complementarity based on joint competence required to compete in the marketplace

▶ Commitment, a reputation based on past performance in collaborative ventures

Establishing the relationship

The second phase of actual relationship-building is likely to require a greater emphasis on relational trust. Most of the people interviewed stressed this. Relational trust becomes significant as the 'glue', the element that helps the alliance move into the third, operational phase. Meetings will be held that highlight protocol and the establishment of personal relationships. Unless this occurs, it will be difficult for parties to align their values, identify the prime purpose for the relationship and work openly through all issues that need to be clarified at the initial development stage. Goodwill and positivity are more likely if relational trust exists alongside calculative trust.

The agreement to jointly venture is ideally driven by similar value systems—those reflected in the cultures of the participating firms. Aligned value systems will provide a common vehicle for moving the collaborative venture forward.

Researchers have shown that what people view as desirable or ideal—their internalised values—conditions the experience of trust and is upheld as a standard to strive for in the future (Gabarro 1978; Butler 1991). A firm whose values system emphasises certain values will strive to achieve those values in its relationship with others. Therefore, it follows that firms with similar value propositions will contribute to the generalised experience of trust and can even create a propensity to trust each other that surpasses specific situations or contingencies. This is the glue that affixes the conditional trust in the ex-ante implementation phase to the evolution to the process-based trust in the ex-post implementation phase.

Relationship maintenance

The operational or ex-post phase of the alliance will be dependent on performance. Hence, calculative trust measures as well as distrust management control systems will be required to ensure both parties believe that their expectations are being fulfilled. Transparency and feedback systems inherently operate to maintain trust or diminish the impact of distrust. These can be structural, such as regular reporting and auditing, as well as psycho-social, such as social gatherings, informal feedback systems and friendship networks.

When the IJV is under implementation, signalling through performance becomes the surrogate for trust. Reciprocal action serves as the basis for mutual commitment (Dwyer *et al.* 1987). Recognition in game theory literature of infinite-horizon games and the empirical demonstration that a 'tit-for-tat' strategy is most optimal under those circumstances (Axelrod 1984) provide further evidence for the role of reciprocity in long-term relational exchange. We suggest that, as an IJV goes through the implementation phase, trust evolves on the basis of reciprocal signalling that conforms to stated intent announced prior to the formation of the IJV.

In this phase the notion of trust is process-based. Repeated interactions allow the participating companies to understand each other's motives and priorities. Part of the process of deciding how much to trust involves finding out in practice about the strategies adopted by one's other partners. Luhmann (1979) argues that a deepening of trust involves a learning process, saying that: 'such learning processes are only complete when the person to be trusted has had opportunities to betray the trust and has not used them' (Luhmann 1979: 45).

Process-based trust creates social capital that enables the trusting party to exercise initiative, assured of the support of the trusted party. Parties in the course of the interaction periodically create, monitor and repair the trust as tensions surface and are resolved (Lewicki and Bunker 1996). These conditions reflect promotive interdependence and co-operation.

Our model (Fig. 1) posits that the evolution of trust can be understood only in the context of the bedrock of 'no trust or absence of trust'. Trust as an instrument of governance contributes to reduction of 'mis-/no trust'. If trust is not present, it has to be created through shared norms and values. In the IJV context it evolves into 'an outcome' from a state of 'pre-condition' (Phase 1: ex-ante; see Fig. 1), in which case it provides an improved basis for ongoing co-operation. Shared norms and values provide a criterion ('glue' in our model) for the selection of partners and in that sense can serve as an instrument of governance.

However, in our view, in the initial phase of contact between the potential IJV partners, the tension between the existence of 'no trust' and 'signals' of trustworthiness (the 'ex-ante' phase) is productive, in the best interests of the interested parties, and is a potential source for the relationship. Switching on the searchlights on the dark areas of mistrust serves the purpose of enabling the emergence of greater trust in collaborative ventures. This is clearly evident in the 'prior enemy' examples in the corporate citizenship arena.

While this model is put forward as a likely common perspective on how relationship development and trust theories interrelate, it is clearly dependent on context and complexity issues outlined above. However, it emerges as a potentially valuable schema to promote awareness of the phases of alliance-building and trust management.

Conclusion

Our paper suggests a dynamic view of the notion of trust in the context of IJVs. IJVs are exchange relationships existing with a significant social component which may be masked or missed in economic explanations of exchange. The sociological perspective captured in the trust construct significantly enhances the explanatory power of the model of governance in the context of IJVs.

Trust theory is becoming recognised as a key issue in a world affected by rapid change and globalisation. It has direct impact on the nature of corporate citizenship. Many of the themes relating to trust outlined above have clear applicability, irrespective of the nature of the alliance. Business–community partnerships can only be enhanced by greater awareness of this field. As corporate citizenship develops as a global movement, international alliances, allegiances and networks are likely to expand. Hence, the issues emerging from this paper will need to be further developed. The significance of positive planning for trust development and the recognition of the impact of distrust open up further fields of research for future work.

References

Axelrod, R. (1984) *The Evolution of Cooperation* (New York: Basic Books).

Baier, A. (1992) 'Ethics as Trusting in Trust: Selections from "Trust and Anti-trust"', in T. Denise and S. Peterfreund (eds.), *Great Traditions in Ethics* (London: Wadsworth Publishing).

Balasubrumanian, N., and D. Kimber (2000) 'Corporate Governance, Reputation and Competitive Credibility', *IIMB Management Review* 12.2 (June 2000): 67-75 .

Barney, J.B. (1991) 'Firm Resources and Sustained Competitive Advantage', *Journal of Management* 17: 99-120.

Blackman, C. (1994) *A Study on Expatriate Australian Managers Working in China* (funded by The Australia–China Chamber of Commerce; Ballarat, Victoria, Australia: University of Ballarat).

Butler, J.K. (1991) 'Toward Understanding and Measuring Conditions of Trust: Evolution of a Conditions of Trust Inventory', *Journal of Management* 17: 643-63.

Collis, D.J., and C.A. Montgomery (1995) 'Competing on Resources: Strategy in the 1990s', *Harvard Business Review*, July/August 1995: 118-28.

Corner, K.R. (1991) 'A Historical Comparison of Resource-Based Theory and Five Schools of Thought within Industrial Organization Economics: Do we have a new theory of the firm?', *Journal of Management* 17: 121-54.

Das, T.K., and Teng Bing-Sheng (1998) 'Between Trust and Control: Developing Confidence in Partner Co-operation in Alliances', *Academy of Management Review* 23.3: 491-512.

Deutsch, M. (1958) 'Trust and Suspicion', *Journal of Conflict Resolution* 2: 265-79.

Dobing, B. (1993) *Building Trust in User–Analyst Relationships* (unpublished doctoral dissertation; Minneapolis: University of Minnesota).

Doney, P.M., J.P. Cannon and M.R. Mullen (1998) 'Understanding the Influence of National Culture on the Development of Trust', *Academy of Management Review* 23.3: 601-20.

Dwyer, F.R., P.H. Schurr and S. Oh (1987) Developing Buyer–Seller Relationships', *Journal of Marketing* 51: 11-27.

Eayrs, M.A. (1993) 'Time, Trust and Hazard: Hairdressers' Symbolic Roles', *Symbolic Interaction* 16.1: 19-37.

Fukuyama, F. (1995) *Trust: The Social Virtues and the Creation of Prosperity* (Harmondsworth, UK: Penguin).

Gabarro, J. (1978) 'The Development of Trust, Influence, and Expectations', in A.G. Athos and J.J. Gabarro (eds.), *Interpersonal Behavior Communications and Understanding in Relationships* (Englewood Cliffs, NJ: Prentice–Hall): 290-303.

Granovetter, M. (1985) 'Economic Action and Social Structure: The Problem of Embeddedness', *American Journal of Sociology* 91: 481-510.

Hagen, J. (1998) 'Trust in Japanese Inter-firm Relations: Institutional Sanctions Matter', *Academy of Management Review* 23.3: 589-600.

Hofstede, G. (1980) *Culture's Consequences: Comparing Values, Behaviors, Institutuions, and Organizations across Nations* (London: Sage).

Hutton, W. (1995) *The State We're In* (London: Jonathan Cape).

Kimber, D., and G. Birchall (1998) 'Values and Trust: The Keys to the Growth of "Social Capital" in Business', *IIMB Management Review*, January–March 1998.

Lewicki, R.J., and B.B. Bunker (1996) 'Developing and Maintaining Trust in Work Relationships', in R.M. Kramer and T.R. Tyler (eds.), *Trust in Organizations: Frontiers of Theory and Research* (Thousand Oaks, CA: Sage): 114-39.

Lewicki, R.J., D.J. McAllister and R.J. Bies (1998) 'Trust and Distrust: New Relationships and Realities', *Academy of Management Review* 23.3: 438-58.

Lewis, J.D., and A.J. Weigert (1985) 'Trust as Social Reality', *Social Forces* 63: 967-85.

Luhmann, N. (1979) *Trust and Power* (Chichester, UK: John Wiley).

Macneil, I.R. (1980) *The New Social Contract* (New Haven, CT: Yale University Press).

Mayer, R.C., J.H. Davis and F.D. Schoorman (1995) 'An Integrative Model of Organisational Trust', *Academy of Management Review* 20: 709-34.

McAllister, D. (1995) 'Affect- and Cognition-Based Trust as Foundations for Interpersonal Co-operation in Organisations', *Academy of Management Journal* 38.1: 24-59.

McKnight, D.H., and N.L. Chervany (1996) *The Meanings of Trust* (MISRC Working Paper Series; St Paul, MN: University of Minnesota Management Information Systems Research Center, www.misrc.umn.edu/wpaper/WorkingPapers/9604.pdf).

Miles, R.E., and W.E.D. Creed (1995) 'Organizational Forms and Managerial Philosophies: A Descriptive and Analytical Review', in L.L. Cummings and B.M. Staw (eds.), *Research in Organizational Behavior* (Vol. XVII; Greenwich, CT: JAI Press): 333-72.

Mishra, A.K. (1996) Organizational Responses to Crisis: The Centrality of Trust', in R.M. Kramer and T.R. Tyler (eds.), *Trust in Organizations: Frontiers of Theory and Research* (Thousand Oaks, CA: Sage): 261-87.

Nooteboom, B. (1999) 'Dynamic Efficiency of Networks', in A. Grandori (ed.), *Inter-firm Networks: Organization and Industrial Competitiveness* (London: Routledge).

Nooteboom, B., H. Berger and N.G. Noorderhaven (1997) 'Effects of Trust and Governance on Relational Risk', *Academy of Management Journal* 40.2: 308-38.

Pankaj Ghemawat (1999) *Strategy and the Business Landscape* (Essex, UK: Pearson Education).

Penrose, E.T. (1959) *The Theory of the Growth of the Firm* (Oxford, UK: Oxford University Press).

Powell, W.W. (1990) 'Neither Market nor Hierarchy', in L.L. Cummings and B.M. Staw (eds.), *Research in Organizational Behavior* (Greenwich, CT: JAI Press): 295-336.

Raghunath, S. (1996a) 'A Strategy for Alliances', *IIMB Management Review*, January–March 1996.

Raghunath, S. (1996b) 'Post-mortem of a Transnational Partnership: Procter & Gamble vs Godrej Soaps', *Business Today*, 22 July–6 August 1996.

Raghunath, S. (1998a) 'Joint Ventures: Does termination mean failure?', *IIMB Management Review*, January–June 1998.

Raghunath, S. (1998b) 'Differing Roles of Company Boards', in N. Balasubrumanian (ed.), *Corporate Boards and Governance* (Macmillan India Ltd).

Ralston Saul, J. (1997) *The Unconscious Civilisation* (The Massey Lecture Series; Harmondsworth, UK: Penguin).

Rempel, J.K., J.G. Holmes and M.P. Zanna (1985) 'Trust in Close Relationships', *Journal of Personality and Social Psychology* 49: 95-112.

Ring, P.S., and A.H. van de Ven (1992) 'Structuring Cooperative Relationships between Organisations', *Strategic Management Journal* 13.7: 483-98.

Rousseau, M., S.B. Sitkin, R.S. Burt and C. Camerer (1998) 'Not so different after all: Cross-discipline View of Trust', *Academy of Management Review* 23.3: 393-404.

Sheppard, B.H., and D.M. Sherman (1998) 'The Grammars of Trust: A Model and General Implications', *Academy of Management Review* 23.3: 422-37.

Shrivastava, H., and S. Venkateswaran (2000) *The Business of Social Responsibility* (Bangalore, India: Books for Change).

Wernerfelt, B. (1984) 'A Resource-Based View of the Firm', *Strategic Management Journal* 5: 171-80.

Whitener, E.M., S.E. Brodt, A.M. Korsgaard and J.M. Werner (1998) 'Managers as Initiators of Trust: An Exchange Relationship Framework for Understanding Managerial Trustworthy Behavior', *Academy of Management Review* 23.3: 513-30.

Williamson, O.E. (1975) *Markets and Hierarchies: Analysis and Antitrust Implications* (New York: Free Press).

Williamson, O.E. (1985) *The Economic Institutions of Capitalism: Firms, Markets, Relational Contracting* (New York: Free Press).

Corporate Volunteering

Ad hoc Interaction or Route to Dialogue and Partnership?

Louise Lee
The Open Polytechnic of New Zealand

Colin Higgins
Massey University, New Zealand

Many businesses demonstrate their role as responsible corporate citizens through involvement in corporate volunteering programmes. There is a growing body of research supporting the view that involvement in corporate volunteering can provide many benefits for business. However, little research has been done on the experience for the employee volunteers or community groups involved. This paper presents the findings of case study research with EDS (NZ), examining the experience of corporate volunteering from a variety of perspectives: business, employee volunteers and the community groups involved. This research reveals that corporate volunteering has the potential to address some of the current issues in the corporate citizenship and corporate social responsibility literature. By raising awareness and generating dialogue between the stakeholders and the different sectors involved, corporate volunteering has the potential to lead to more sustained community–business partnerships. Corporate volunteering may also provide an important mechanism for business organisations to interact and engage with the local communities in which they operate, in an era when multinational corporations are struggling for legitimacy in a globalised economy.

- Corporate volunteering
- Partnership
- Corporate citizenship
- Asia–Pacific
- Globalisation
- Multinational corporations

Louise Lee is a lecturer in management at the Open Polytechnic of New Zealand teaching business management at undergraduate level. Her doctoral research seeks to explore the process of developing effective partnerships between business and community organisations and understand specific challenges facing cross-sectoral partnerships.

✉ School of Management, The Open Polytechnic of New Zealand, 86 Wyndrum Avenue, Lower Hutt, Wellington, New Zealand

🖥 leelou@topnz.ac.nz

🌐 www.topnz.ac.nz

Colin Higgins is a lecturer in management at Massey University, New Zealand. As well as being an associate member of NZ Businesses for Social Responsibility, he is also an affiliated scholar of the Corporate Citizenship Research Unit at Deakin University in Australia where he is undertaking his doctoral research.

✉ Department of Management, Private Bag 11-222, Palmerston North, New Zealand

🖥 C.P.Higgins@massey.ac.nz

🌐 www.massey.ac.nz

THE PUBLIC ENVIRONMENT IN WHICH BUSINESS OPERATES TODAY IS FAR different from that of just 20 years ago. For instance, there have been dramatic and far-reaching changes in the perceptions of the relationship between business and society. This has been reflected in the literature. For example, since the 1960s ,questions have been raised about the legitimacy of the prevailing market system, and the effect that this has on business's relationship with society. Similarly, debate concerning the 'correct' role of business in society has raged since the 1970s. Additionally, the literature throughout this time has been dotted with numerous case studies of how businesses have related to their communities. More recently, issues such as globalisation and the role and responsibility of multinational corporations have been receiving significant attention.

One particular way in which businesses relate to their communities, which is well established and reflected in case studies, is corporate volunteering. Much has been written describing the extent and the variety of activities that corporate volunteering encompasses, particularly in the US and UK, and the many benefits that involvement can provide for the business. However, there has been little research done on the experience for the employee volunteers and community groups involved.

What does appear to be emerging in the literature, however, is the view that an effective business response to societal issues and a meaningful contribution to a civil society require more than just piecemeal, ad hoc interactions with the community. Literature emerging in the 1990s has been focusing on a 'new paradigm' of business, emphasising linked prosperity and partnerships between business, government and society to create a good and civil society.

This paper reports on a case study of corporate volunteering with the New Zealand arm of multinational computing firm, EDS. It examines the perceptions of corporate volunteering from the perspective of the business, employees and the community groups involved. The findings of this study suggest that corporate volunteering generates considerable benefits for all three groups. The findings also suggest that community groups do in fact desire a more sustained commitment from business organisations than is frequently provided by corporate volunteering. The authors suggest, however, that corporate volunteering, by providing opportunities for sharing, dialogue and raising awareness of the perspectives of different sectors, offers the potential to contribute to a number of current and important issues in the corporate social responsibility and corporate citizenship literature.

The importance of building on the benefits of corporate volunteering to achieve a more sustained community–business involvement is emphasised, as is the potential for corporate volunteering to provide opportunities for engagement with local communities in the areas where corporations operate. Engagement with local communities is becoming an increasingly important need as globalisation has increased the size and reach of many corporations and diminished corporations' ties to local communities.

After providing an overview of the methodology employed in this study, this paper highlights key aspects of the literature relating to corporate social responsibility, corporate citizenship, corporate volunteering and partnership in the Asia–Pacific region. A brief description of the corporate volunteering programme at EDS, both locally and internationally, is then discussed before the results and conclusions of the current study are presented.

Literature review

The Western perspective

Despite current fascination in the press in New Zealand and elsewhere about the social responsibility of business, corporate social responsibility and corporate citizenship is largely a Western phenomenon, and the attention to this issue in the literature is not new. Writers such as Thurow (1966), Galbraith (1972) and others have focused on the degree to which the priorities and outcomes of the current Western capitalist model create an environment for business that has damaging consequences for society. During the 1970s and 1980s, attention in the literature appeared to focus on the issues arising out of the relationship between business and society. See, for example, Friedman 1970; Beesley and Evans 1978; Jones 1974; Steiner and Steiner 1972; Berger 1981; Carroll 1979; and Dalton and Cosier 1982. The late 1980s and early 1990s saw a proliferation of case studies on the ways in which business interacted directly with the community, and debate concerning the correct role of business in society. See, for example, Drucker 1984; Evans and Freeman 1988; Donaldson 1982; Buchholz 1991; Bowie 1991; and Kerr 1996. Lately, protest action in Seattle, Prague, Melbourne and Davos during World Economic Forum and World Trade Organisation meetings have raised issues of legitimacy for multinational corporations and concern for new business and society issues arising out of globalisation (see Zadek 1998).

The Asian–Pacific perspective

The attention to corporate social responsibility and corporate citizenship in the Asia–Pacific region is relatively limited, but interest appears to be increasing. This is evidenced by the emergence of centres and associations addressing corporate citizenship and corporate social responsibility. The Asian Institute of Management's Centre for Corporate Responsibility, which recently held a Corporate Responsibility Week in Manila (Basilio 2000), and the Japan Society for Business Ethics (Wokutch 1990) are two such examples.

In addition to this, there appear to be a number of drivers of corporate social responsibility and corporate citizenship in the Asia–Pacific context. The responses of corporations and the issues of concern, however, do not appear to be consistent across the region. In some of the less developed regions (such as Malaysia and the Philippines) the issues of corporate social responsibility and corporate citizenship are emerging out of recognition of the price of unrestrained and unregulated economic growth (Teoh and Thong 1984; Garchitorena 2000; Basilio 2000). In Japan, interest appears to centre on the movement of Western corporations into the region, and movements of Asian corporations into the West. This has resulted in the translation of current Western business practices (including corporate social responsibility and corporate citizenship) into the Asian context and the emulation of Western business practices by Asian business setting up operations in the West (Wokutch 1990; Selwyn 1992). It is important in this context, however, to consider the observations of Antal (1985), Wokutch (1990) and Ang and Leong (2000) that business–society interactions are rooted in deeply seated cultural norms and traditions. Antal (1985), for example, suggests 'the need to understand the socio-political environment, as well as the organisational culture of particular businesses, in order to understand the way that corporate social responsibility is shaped' (quoted in Moore and Richardson 1990: 205).

Corporate volunteering

One common way in which business organisations interact with their communities in the West (and to a lesser extent in the East), which deserves further consideration in this context, is corporate volunteering. Much has been written describing the experience of corporate volunteering from a business perspective. For example, the Conference Board (1993), Business in the Community (1993), Caudron (1994), Tuffrey (1995) and Carroll (1996) all discuss business benefits of corporate volunteering programmes. These include developing better workforces, enhancing corporate reputations and investing in the communities in which their businesses trade. Tuffrey (1995) and Quirke (1999) expand on the human resource benefits that corporate volunteering can provide, arguing that corporate volunteering offers opportunities for challenge and skills development for staff and has a positive impact on staff morale and motivation. Community involvement supported and encouraged by the business, they argue, is seen as a way to build a sense of identification with the values and goals of the business.

The literature focusing on employee volunteers' experiences appears to be less extensive. Tuffrey (1995) and Quirke (1998) touch on the reasons why people choose to participate in corporate volunteering programmes. These reasons include a desire to make a difference to the community, enhancing work performance and meeting other people. Post et al. (1996) suggest that employees can develop leadership skills and other useful workplace skills by participating in corporate volunteering programmes.

From the perspective of the community groups, there are even fewer studies. Tuffrey (1995) suggests that programmes such as short placements for staff in community organisations, to work on precisely defined assignments, or mentoring schemes between business and community organisations, can help to provide expertise to community organisations (see also Business in the Community 1993). Quirke (1998) highlighted benefits for the community groups at two levels: the individual community organisation and the wider societal level. Finally, Business in the Community (1993) suggests that corporate volunteering can offer the potential for mutually beneficial partnerships to develop between community organisations and business. For these partnerships to be sustainable, however, a climate of trust and an understanding of what each hopes to gain must be fostered.

Recently, the corporate citizenship and corporate social responsibility literature has focused on this idea of partnership. In theorising emerging approaches to business, concepts such as reciprocal relationships, partnerships, dialogue, diversity and inclusivity are common (RSA 1996; Elkington 1997; McIntosh et al. 1998).

All of these writers stress that the key to an effective business contribution to the community requires developing mutual, beneficial partnerships between business and community groups. Birch (1999), for example, stresses that long-term interactive partnerships 'rather than short term transactive relationships' (Birch 1999: 7) are the key to developing social coalition. Similarly, Kanter (1999) suggests that 'new paradigm partnerships' (Kanter 1999: 124) have the potential to attack stubborn social problems and to produce faster innovations and transformations. Birch (1999) also summarises a Danish programme called 'New Partnership for Social Cohesion' launched by Karen Jespersen, Minister for Social Affairs, in 1998, which stresses mutuality, reciprocity and sustained participation.

While these writers acknowledge the contribution that transactional relationships, such as corporate volunteering and philanthropy, can make to the community, they tend to argue that these interactions are ineffective. They have the tendency, according to Birch (1999), to be fragile and can lead to one-sided relationships of dependency. Long-term, reciprocal and mutually beneficial partnerships can help to develop more sustainable outcomes from business interactions with the community.

It is important to recognise, however, that the development of partnerships between business and the community can be difficult and problematic (Murphy 2000). Additionally, these judgements about transactional relationships such as corporate volunteering are made in light of limited research on the perceptions of the stakeholders involved.

Effective partnerships require stakeholder inclusion; an understanding of the expectations of the various parties involved in the partnership is important if the partnership is to be effective. Therefore, there is a need to understand the expectations of employee volunteers and community groups as well as understanding the business case to support corporate volunteering.

Methodology

Previous research on corporate volunteering has largely described the experiences of businesses in the US and UK. In this study, a case study approach was adopted in order to explore the practices and experiences of a business organisation actively engaged in corporate volunteering, in New Zealand, from the perspective of the business, employee volunteers and the community groups involved. A two-stage approach to the research was adopted using both qualitative and quantitative techniques.

The first stage of the research focused on gathering data through interviews and focus groups to better understand the phenomenon of corporate volunteering within the New Zealand context from a variety of perspectives.

Interviews were held with EDS senior management responsible for the organisation and management of the corporate volunteering initiatives. In order to probe and explore issues relating to employees' perceptions of the corporate volunteering initiatives supported by EDS, a random sample of 20 EDS employees who had been involved in EDS's corporate volunteering programmes were invited to attend a focus group session. Two focus group sessions were held with 12 EDS employees attending in total. Interviews were also held with four representatives from a sample of community organisations that had participated in EDS's corporate volunteering initiatives in the previous year.

An interview was also held with the Employees in the Community programme manager from the Wellington Volunteer Centre. The key purpose of the interview was to gain an understanding of the role of the Wellington Volunteer Centre in supporting businesses such as EDS to become involved in employee volunteering.

Data gathered during stage one was then used to design a questionnaire in stage two, which investigated the perceptions of the employees and community groups involved in corporate volunteering. A self-administered questionnaire was e-mailed to a proportional stratified random sample of 78 EDS employees throughout New Zealand. The sample was chosen from population of 212 staff who had been involved in EDS corporate volunteering initiatives in the previous year. From the 78 questionnaires e-mailed, 16 were not returned, 18 were returned uncompleted as those people had since left EDS and 44 others were returned completed. The response rate of those who received the questionnaire was 73%. A random sample of five community groups was also sent a questionnaire. Three of these groups responded.

Description of the EDS programme

EDS (NZ) is a subsidiary of EDS, one of the world's leading outsourcer, integrator and business process management service providers. In New Zealand EDS employs over

1,100 people and provides services in four key areas: systems and technology services; business process management; management consulting; and e-business.

Corporate volunteering has been a key EDS priority since 1986 in the United States. In 1993 EDS Global Volunteer Day was developed in response to a desire by the company to expand the spirit of volunteerism as the employee base of the company grew abroad. Key objectives of the Global Volunteer Day programme are to have a positive impact on local communities by recognising the commitment of employees' volunteer efforts in local communities and by mobilising new employee volunteers as well as families, friends and clients. During October 2000 EDS volunteers donated more than 38,800 hours working on more than 400 projects in 20 countries including New Zealand, Australia, Singapore, Thailand, China and the Philippines in the Asia–Pacific region.

In New Zealand EDS has three distinct corporate volunteering initiatives: Global Volunteer Day, Net Day and the Community Grants Scheme. Global Volunteer Day involves staff voluntarily spending one day per year, usually in the month of October, doing 'hands-on' work in the community. For Net Day, technical staff volunteer their time to install computer networks in Wellington schools. The Community Grants Scheme involves employee nomination of non-profit organisations for a $500 cash grant with allocation made by a selection panel of EDS staff.

EDS (NZ) provides the following institutional support for its corporate volunteering initiatives:

▶ A corporate volunteering co-ordinator to facilitate employee community involvement

▶ A staff release-time policy

▶ Company endorsement

This paper discusses the business's, employee volunteers', and the community groups' experiences in the corporate volunteering programmes undertaken by EDS (NZ).

Results and discussion

The business perception of corporate volunteering

EDS, as a business organisation, viewed corporate volunteering primarily as a way to express its desire to be a good corporate citizen. While also acknowledging that corporate volunteering could provide human resource benefits, and an opportunity to develop a positive public profile and an enhanced reputation, these were not seen as key drivers for EDS's involvement in corporate volunteering.

Expression of corporate citizenship
The key objective for EDS in its corporate volunteering initiatives was to provide a tangible and visible expression of corporate citizenship. For example, EDS management consistently stressed the notion of commitment to community as the key reason for the corporate volunteering programme.

The selection of corporate volunteering as the vehicle by which EDS demonstrates its commitment to being a good corporate citizen appears to be driven by a desire to include employees in the corporate citizenship process. The corporate volunteering pro-grammes in place at EDS are organised to facilitate and foster employee involvement and ownership. For example, the EDS corporate volunteering co-ordinator indicated that there is an emphasis on employee-led initiatives in the selection of projects for Global Volunteer Day. She encourages staff who have connections with community groups to suggest possible projects. She then follows these suggestions through to completion or staff may manage the projects themselves if they wish. One staff member, for instance, who is involved with an environmental group, sourced and co-ordinated projects involving over 30 employees with this community group for Global Volunteer Day.

Human resource benefits

EDS management also recognised the potential that corporate volunteering could provide for team-building and building staff morale. For example, Global Volunteer Day was strongly promoted as providing opportunities to work in teams in a non-working setting, and one newly appointed manager specifically used corporate volunteering as a means to strengthen teamwork.

EDS management also acknowledged the potential for corporate volunteering to develop employee pride in the organisation. However, no formal assessment measuring staff attitudes to EDS as a result of community involvement has been initiated as yet, indicating that these are not considered to be significant motives in the corporate volunteering process.

Additionally, while research suggests that corporate volunteering has the potential for employee skill enhancement, as programmes are presently structured at EDS these opportunities appear limited. The majority of staff are involved in community projects using general non-work-related skills rather than technical work-based skills. This further strengthens the resolve that corporate volunteering is viewed primarily as a corporate citizenship exercise.

Public profile

Corporate volunteering was also perceived as providing opportunities to raise awareness of what EDS is and what it does in the wider community. While these public relations benefits were recognised, like the human resource benefits they were not seen as key drivers for supporting corporate volunteering, as no measurement of these aspects take place, and little emphasis is placed on them when corporate volunteering is planned and discussed.

The employee volunteers' perceptions of corporate volunteering

The employee volunteers perceived involvement in corporate volunteering initiatives primarily as a way to contribute personally to the community and to gain an understanding and awareness of community issues. In addition to this, the potential for personal gain was also a key benefit cited by many of the respondents. Business benefits were also recognised, but they did not appear to hold as prominent a position for employee volunteers. These results are summarised in Figure 1.

Personal contribution to the community

The desire to help and contribute to the community was a key perception that employee volunteers had of their corporate volunteering experience. For example, statements such as 'a good way to help people' and 'a good way of helping a specific community group' have the highest mean scores, as indicated in Figure 1.

The main types of contribution that employee volunteers thought they made to the community included practical assistance, but opportunities to foster greater awareness and understanding of wider community issues were also significant outcomes perceived by the employee volunteers. For example, volunteers described learning about community organisations that operate in different ways and that face many different pressures compared with a large, for-profit organisation such as EDS.

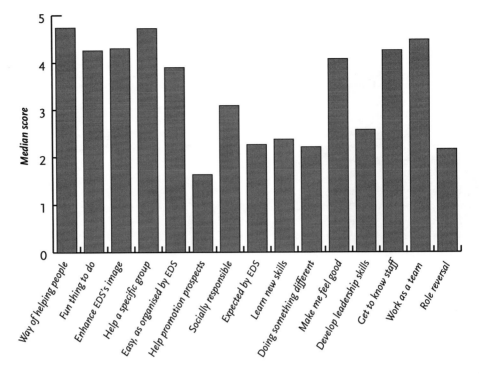

Figure 1 EMPLOYEE VOLUNTEERS' PERCEPTIONS OF BENEFITS OF CORPORATE VOLUNTEERING

Potential for personal gain

Employee volunteers also appeared to have a strong perception that they gained some personal benefits from participating in the corporate volunteering programme. A number of the participants in the focus group sessions commented about gaining a personal sense of satisfaction 'the feel-good, nice-warm-glow stuff'. As indicated in Figure 1, these personal benefits included having fun with family and friends and raised self-esteem.

Interestingly, employee volunteers' perceptions of personal gain appeared to be based around personal satisfaction, rather than the development of specific skills. For example, Figure 1 indicates that employees did not perceive that they had learned new skills or developed leadership skills.

Potential for business benefits

Employee volunteers also perceived that EDS would gain from supporting and encouraging staff to become involved in corporate volunteering. As indicated in Figure 1, these benefits include opportunities to develop staff through team-building, enhancing EDS's reputation and getting to know colleagues in a different environment.

Having said this, however, it seems that the employee volunteers viewed the exercise more as a personal exercise, and less as a business exercise. For example, a significant number of employee volunteers participated in corporate volunteering in their own time rather than work time. Additionally, some employee volunteers were unaware of the staff release-time policy, and others perceived difficulties organising teams of volunteers during work time with the nature of existing work schedules. Furthermore, both EDS management and employee volunteers expressed dissatisfaction with what they perceived as presently inadequate levels of participation from EDS senior management.

The community group representatives' perceptions of corporate volunteering

The community group representatives involved in the EDS corporate volunteering programme perceived a number of useful benefits that could be derived from the programme. While one of the obvious benefits of corporate volunteering was the practical assistance provided to complete a variety of tasks, it was also acknowledged that corporate volunteering provided the community group with an opportunity to raise awareness of the particular societal issues they were involved in addressing. Additionally, the potential to raise the profile of their organisations through association with a well-known organisation was also cited as a significant benefit. Some community groups also saw corporate volunteering as a means of developing long-term, mutual partnerships with business organisations.

Practical assistance

Community group representatives perceived that Global Volunteer Day provides a good mechanism for completing necessary tasks and in doing so helping the organisation to achieve its goals. For example, community organisations involved had received assistance with general maintenance, gardening, conservation work, a trip to the zoo with retirement home residents, a wine trail with Foundation for the Blind clients and taking IHC (intellectually handicapped children) clients dragon-boating.

Awareness-raising

For many of the community organisations, fundamental to the existence of the organisation was an educative role on a variety of issues such as sight impairment, environmental awareness, intellectual disabilities and others. Representatives from two community groups involved in Global Volunteer Day discussed the opportunities that corporate volunteering provided to expose the wider community to the causes their organisations promote. Global Volunteer Day projects they had been involved in required specialised training before the activities took place. These training sessions and the Global Volunteer Day activities themselves were seen as providing valuable opportunities to break down myths and barriers and help participants to get involved in issues they may have been unaware of.

Raising public profile

A majority of the community group representatives also perceived that involvement helped the community group to raise its profile and generate community support for the work that they were involved in. Ways to work together with the business to achieve this were seen as particularly important for one organisation. This community organisation is involved in a project on a significant area of public land. As such they need to demonstrate to funders that there is community support and 'buy-in' for the work of the Trust. Being part of EDS's Global Volunteer Day and publicising this was perceived as being very important for the Trust.

Development of mutual partnerships

For one community group representative, a five-year involvement with Global Volunteer Day had provided a strong basis for a mutually beneficial partnership to develop. The representative from this community organisation spoke of the need for both EDS and the community organisation to nurture the partnership with time and energy. Dialogue on what both parties wanted from the relationship was necessary if it was to be an effective working partnership. She expressed a desire to extend this partnership to gain access to specific business skills, particularly in terms of marketing and promotion.

Another community group that had been involved with Global Volunteer Day for three years also expressed an interest in further developing the relationship they had established with EDS, and was considering ways that they could build and strengthen the partnership for mutual benefit.

Comments from community group representatives stressed the importance of establishing mutually beneficial relationships. While they recognised that the needs of EDS and the community organisations were quite different, with time and communication, the partnership could grow and develop.

Conclusion

This study of corporate volunteering reveals a number of important benefits for all three key stakeholder groups involved. Corporate volunteering enables business to make a tangible contribution to the community, involve their employees, and to receive some additional benefits in the form of team-building and employee pride. The employee volunteers gain an opportunity to contribute to the community and to learn about wider community issues. The community groups, in addition to receiving practical assistance, fulfil their educative role and also raise awareness of the various causes their organisations represent. Corporate volunteering provides opportunities for sharing, dialogue and understanding between different sectors to develop. This offers a potentially useful contribution to a number of areas of current corporate citizenship and corporate social responsibility interest.

While the corporate volunteering initiatives in place at EDS have not at this stage developed into extensive, mutually beneficial partnerships, this research reveals that the benefits derived are meaningful, welcomed and positive for the groups involved. Corporate volunteering therefore has the potential to develop partnership opportunities between business and the community.

In addition to this, corporate volunteering provides opportunities for sharing, dialogue and understanding, allowing business organisations to interact and engage in the communities in which they operate. This is becoming important as evidenced by growing unrest over the darker side of unregulated and unrestrained economic development and an increasingly globalised business environment.

It is also important to consider that business–society interactions reflect varying social, cultural and organisational values. Further research to better understand the socio-political environments and organisational cultures shaping business–society interactions is needed in order to assess the degree to which these New Zealand case study findings can be generalised into different contexts such as the Asia–Pacific region.

However, notwithstanding these potential contributions, and the importance of further research in these areas, the practice of corporate volunteering provides a number of useful and important benefits in its own right.

References

Ang, S.H., and S.M. Leong (2000) 'Out of the Mouths of Babes: Business Ethics and Youth in Asia', *Journal of Business Ethics*, November 2000: 129-44.

Antal, A. (1985) 'Institutionalizing Corporate Social Responsiveness: Lessons from the MIGROS Experience', *Research in Corporate Social Performance and Policy* 7: 229-49.

Basilio, R. (2000) 'Big business incorporates social responsibility in their missions', *Business World*, 7 July 2000: 9-10.

Beesley, M., and T. Evans (1978) *Corporate Social Responsibility: A Reassessment* (London: Croom Helm).

Berger, P.L. (1981) 'New Attack on the Legitimacy of Business', *Harvard Business Review* 59.5: 82-89.

Birch, D. (1999) 'Achieving Social Coalition: Some Key Principles of Partnership', *Achieving Social Coalition Seminar* (CCRU Deakin University and Epoch Foundation; Melbourne: RMIT, 3 June 1999).

Bowie, N. (1991) 'New Directions in Corporate Social Responsibility', *Business Horizons* 34.4: 56-65.

Buchholz, R.A. (1991) 'Corporate Responsibility and the Good Society: From Economics to Ecology', *Business Horizons* 34.4: 19-31.

Business in the Community (1993) *Investing in People* (London: Business in the Community).

Carroll, A.B. (1979) 'A Three Dimensional Conceptual Model of Corporate Performance', *Academy of Management Review* 4: 497-505.

Carroll, A.B. (1996) *Business and Society* (Cincinnati, OH: South-Western Publishing).

Caudron, S. (1994) 'Volunteer efforts offer low-cost training', *Personnel Journal* 73.6: 38-44.

Conference Board (1993) *Corporate Volunteering Programmes: Benefits to Business* (New York: Conference Board).

Dalton, D.R., and R.A. Cosier (1982) 'The Four Faces of Social Responsibility', *Business Horizons* 25.3: 19-27.

Donaldson, T. (1982) 'The Social Contract: Norms for a Corporate Conscience', in W.M. Hoffman and R.E. Frederick (eds.), *Business Ethics: Readings and Cases in Corporate Morality* (New York: McGraw–Hill): 65-91.

Drucker, P. (1984) 'The New Meaning of Corporate Social Responsibility', *California Management Review* 26.2: 53-63.

Elkington, J. (1997) *Cannibals with Forks: The Triple Bottom Line of 21st Century Business* (Oxford, UK: Capstone Publishing).

Evans, W.M., and R.E. Freeman (1988) 'A Stakeholder Theory of the Modern Corporation: Kantian Capitalism', in W.M. Hoffman and R.E. Frederick (eds.), *Business Ethics: Readings and Cases in Corporate Morality* (New York: McGraw–Hill): 145-57.

Friedman, M. (1970) 'The social responsibility of business is to increase its profits', in W.M. Hoffman and R.E. Frederick (eds.), *Business Ethics: Readings and Cases in Corporate Morality* (New York: McGraw–Hill): 137-41.

Galbraith, J.L. (1972) 'The Emerging Public Corporation', in G.A. Steiner and J.S. Steiner (eds.), *Issues in Business and Society* (New York: Random House): 54-56.

Garchitorena, V. (2000) 'Editorial. One Voice: Corporate Responsibilities', *Business World*, 17 August 2000: 3.

Jones, R.H. (1974) 'What is the future of the corporation? An address to the Detroit Economic Club', in G.A. Steiner and J.S. Steiner (eds.), *Issues in Business and Society* (New York: Random House): 534-43.

Kanter, R.M. (1999) 'From Spare Change to Real Change', *Harvard Business Review* 77.3: 122-32.

Kerr, R. (1996) 'The Meaning of Corporate Social Responsibility', conference paper presented at *AIESEC Corporate Social Responsibility Seminar*, 3 June 1996, Auckland (Auckland: New Zealand Business Roundtable).

McIntosh, M., D. Leipziger, K. Jones and G. Coleman (1998) *Corporate Citizenship: Successful Strategies for Responsible Companies* (London: Pitman).

Moore, C., and J. Richardson (1990) 'The Politics and Practice of Corporate Responsibility in Great Britain', in L. Preston (ed.), *International and Comparative Corporate and Society Research* (Greenwich, CT: JAI Press): 203-36.

Murphy, J. (2000) 'Business–Community Partnerships: Fact or Fantasy?', *Mornington Peninsula Community Connections, Broken Hill Community Round Table*, 26 February 2000, Broken Hill (Broken Hill, NSW, Australia: Community Connections).

Post, J., W. Frederick, A. Lawrence and J. Weber (1996) *Business and Society: Corporate Strategy, Public Policy, Ethics* (New York: McGraw–Hill).

Quirke, D. (1998) *Corporate Volunteering: The Potential Way Forward* (report prepared as part of a Churchill Fellowship; Wellington, New Zealand: Department of Internal Affairs).

Quirke, D. (1999) 'Employee Volunteering', *Human Resources*, February 1999: 2-4.

RSA (Royal Society for the Encouragement of Arts, Manufacture and Commerce) (1996) *Tomorrow's Company* (London: RSA).

Selwyn, M. (1992) 'A Reputation for Success', *Asian Business* 28.5: 24-36.

Steiner, G.A., and J.S. Steiner (eds.) (1972) *Issues in Business and Society* (New York: Random House, 2nd edn).

Teoh, H.Y., and G. Thong (1984) 'Another Look at Corporate Social Responsibility and Reporting: An Empirical Study in a Developing Country', *Accounting, Organisations and Society* 9.2: 189-206.

Thurow, L. (1966) *The Future of Capitalism: How Today's Economic Forces Shape Tomorrow's World* (St Leonards, Australia: Allen & Unwin).

Tuffrey, M. (1995) *Employees and the Community* (London: PRIMA Europe).

Wokutch, R. (1990) 'Corporate Social Responsibility Japanese Style', *Academy of Management Executive* 4.2: 56-74.

Zadek, S. (1998) 'Balancing Performance, Ethics, and Accountability', *Journal of Business Ethics* 17.13: 1421-41.

Social Reporting and Australian Banks

Endorsement or Pretence to the Triple Bottom Line?*

Mary E. Sweeney
University of Melbourne, Australia

Anona Armstrong, Gary O'Donovan and Maree Fitzpatrick
Victoria University, Australia

Banks represent an important industry in Australia owing to their size and overall impact on the economy. A banking sector characterised by good corporate citizens, behaving in a socially responsible manner, will benefit all Australians. The question posed in this paper is not whether banks can be considered good corporate citizens per se, but rather whether they report their citizenship behaviour in an open and honest way. Accounting criteria applied to evaluate the quality of banking reports include relevance, freedom from bias and understandability.

Findings suggest that banks are beginning to recognise that they have a responsibility to a broader group of stakeholders than shareholders alone, but, with a few notable exceptions, there is little evidence to suggest they have gone beyond the rhetoric stage. The current state of play is highlighted, areas in need of reform are identified and some examples of good practice are provided for other banks to follow.

● Corporate social responsibility

● Triple-bottom-line reporting

● Banking sector

● Australia

● Quality of reporting

● Stakeholders

Dr Mary Sweeney is a Senior Fellow in the Centre of Financial Studies at the University of Melbourne. She majored in accounting and economics and has a PhD in finance.

✉ Centre of Financial Studies, Faculty of Economics and Commerce, University of Melbourne, Victoria 3010, Australia

💻 msweeney@unimelb.edu.au

Dr Anona Armstrong is the Director of the Business Ethics Research Unit at Victoria University and is an Associate Professor in the School of Management.

✉ Business Ethics Research Unit, Victoria University, Box 14428, MCMC, Melbourne, Victoria 8001, Australia

💻 anona.armstrong@vu.edu.au

Dr Gary O'Donovan is a Senior Lecturer in Accounting and Finance at Victoria University. His PhD was in the area of Corporate Environmental Accounting and Reporting.

✉ Victoria University, Box 14428, MCMC, Melbourne, Victoria 8001, Australia

💻 gary.odonovan@vu.edu.au

Ms Maree Fitzpatrick is a member of the Business Ethics Research Unit at Victoria University. She has recently been awarded a PhD scholarship and plans to examine corporate social reporting in Australia.

✉ Business Ethics Research Unit, Victoria University, Box 14428, MCMC, Melbourne, Victoria 8001, Australia

💻 fitzpatrick@vu.edu.au

* The authors would like to thank Victoria University for a seeding grant provided to support this project. Comments and feedback provided by participants at an Evaluation Society and Victoria University Business Ethics Seminar are gratefully acknowledged.

H OW THE WHEEL TURNS. AT THE EMERGENCE OF THE 20TH CENTURY, corporations were pushing for citizenship rights (Waddell in Altman and Vivader-Cohen 2000: 6). Today, at the dawn of the 21st century, corporations are again being challenged to fulfil their citizenship duties. The view that the purpose of business is to enrich society as a whole, not only management and shareholders, is gaining in credibility (Solomon 1992). The view that 'corporate social responsibility consists of making as much money for their shareholders as possible' (Friedman 1962: 133) is no longer valid. Global corporations are expected to be good corporate citizens and accept social responsibility towards a broader base than shareholders alone.

Corporate social responsibility (CSR) refers to 'the obligations of businessmen to pursue those policies, to make those decisions, or to follow those lines of action which are desirable in terms of the objectives and values of our society' (Buchholz 1995: 23). It is the continuing commitment by business to behave ethically and contribute to economic development while improving the quality of life of the workforce and their families as well as the community and society at large. In particular, according to the World Business Council for Sustainable Development (WBCSD 1999) this means acting with responsibility in its relationships with other stakeholders, not just shareholders. There are various opinions concerning who the corporate stakeholders are (Freeman 1984; Davenport 2000). Watts and Holme (1999) list stakeholders as those affected by or those affecting a business's activities, including representatives from labour organisations, academia, church, indigenous peoples, human rights groups, government and non-government organisations. This paper takes the view, based on Estes (1999), that stakeholders include employees and contractors, customers and suppliers, the community and society (including the natural environment) as well as shareholders.

Husted and Allen (2000) explore the nexus between corporate citizenship and CSR. They claim the concept of corporate citizenship is closely related to CSR, except corporate citizenship is a proactive concept that has emerged from the political science literature, whereas CSR is a reactive concept that has emerged from the sociological literature. This paper is concerned with corporate citizenship and CSR in a broad sense that goes beyond the single bottom line of financial responsibilities. These terms are used interchangeably throughout the paper.

An Australian study by Glazebrook (1999) indicated several key areas influencing a company's corporate citizenship profile: social and environmental responsibility, governance, ethics, sponsorship, stakeholder relations and partnerships. There is evidence to suggest that corporate citizenship is influenced by culture and size of the company and the industry in which it operates (Zadek et al. 1997; Shiraz 1998; KPMG 1999; Maignan and Ferrell 2000; Adams 2000; Spence and Lozano 2000). The focus of this paper is on large corporations in the banking industry within an Australian cultural context.

Australian corporations, especially the banks, have been slow to accept changes in expectations regarding their role as corporate citizens. The viewpoint that corporations existed solely to maximise shareholder wealth was still prevalent in Australia in the 1970s and to a lesser extent in the 1980s. A more enlightened viewpoint, following the excesses in Australia in the 1980s, emerged in speeches by the Australian Prime Minister in the late 1990s. His argument, that business needs to earn its licence to operate in a community by being more generous to that community (Birch 2000), follows overseas trends. Estes (1996b, 1999), for example, claims that corporations were first chartered to serve the public purpose, and in return were granted certain privileges (for example, limited liability, transport, telecommunications and other infrastructure). In exchange for 'privileges', there are expectations from society of responsible behaviour. That is, in order to be good corporate citizens, corporations need to take their social responsibilities seriously and consider the wellbeing of all stakeholders, not shareholders exclusively.

Failure to be accountable to all stakeholders and an over-reliance on single-bottom-line financial reporting is a problem that has plagued accounting reports for decades (Sweeney and Estes 2000). These traditional economic and financial reporting inadequacies have led to various efforts to combine financial, social and environmental elements into a triple-bottom-line reporting framework (Elkington 1997). Estes (1996a, 1996b, 1999) developed the Sunshine Standards, which identified information required by customers, workers, communities and society at large. According to the WBCSD (1999), effective management of CSR demands monitoring, measuring and reporting of performance against generally accepted indicators. The Sunshine Standards provide a framework for classifying the indicators of information that customers, workers, community and society at large may need for rational decision-making (se the Appendix).

There are many possible reasons for reporting CSR activities. One reason is a desire to be perceived by outside parties as operating legitimately within the bounds and norms of society (O'Donovan 1999; Deegan 2000). Hooghiemstra (2000) claims that legitimacy theory is currently the dominating perspective in CSR reporting. However, the rationale for CSR reporting in Australian banks is beyond the scope of this study. The focus is on the quality of *what* they report, rather than *why* they report it.

The view taken in this paper is that good corporate citizenship requires adherence to six ethical principles: dignity, equity, prudence, honesty, openness and goodwill (Francis 2000). Adherence to principles of equity *per se*, or dignity, prudence and goodwill, are not being evaluated in this paper. The concern is rather with the principles of honesty and openness (transparency is another term often used in this context). Are corporations open and honest in the way they *report* information on CSR issues and corporate citizenship generally? The purpose is to evaluate whether members of the Australian banking industry report their CSR activities in an open and honest way.

The next section reviews the literature on CSR reporting and is followed by a description of the evaluation framework, the data and methods used. Evidence of performance against evaluation criteria is provided in the subsequent section. The final section provides a summary, conclusions and directions for further research. Limitations in the analysis are also discussed in this final section.

CSR reporting

Although Australian corporations still have a long way to go to reach balanced and sustainable value creation, business leaders are beginning to understand that they have to satisfy a broader group of interested stakeholders who have influence and rights, including a right to CSR information (Birch and Glazebrook 2000). Corporations reporting CSR information in an open, honest and transparent way are meeting one of the requirements of being a good corporate citizen. It is unrealistic to demand commitment from employees if the future of their own jobs is shrouded in secrecy, or to ask suppliers to comply with codes of conduct if the companies themselves have a less systematic, rigorous approach to disclosure (Zadek *et al.* 1997).

All publicly listed companies are required to produce an annual report for their shareholders. Increasingly, the annual report, in addition to financial reports, also includes information on the social and environmental aspects of a business (Gibson and O'Donovan 2000). The report must contain financial information, corporate governance information and a company's policy on the establishment and maintenance of appropriate ethical standards. Providing CSR information of interest to stakeholders other than shareholders, however, is voluntary rather than mandatory.

Some would argue that there is no need for CSR disclosures because the free market regulates corporations. If corporations do not provide good products at a fair price, they will not survive. In a free society, with perfect markets, complete and full information on the activities of corporations would be freely available to all stakeholders. The market would then be the arbiter of whether they should prosper or not. Unfortunately, conditions for effective markets (i.e. perfect information) are not met.

Some CSR theorists claim further regulation is required to make corporations more accountable, equitable and efficient (Elkington 1997). Corporations are accountable, in Australia and elsewhere, through various regulations requiring them to report to a plethora of agencies on the performance of numerous activities of interest to stakeholders. An example of how behaviour can be changed by more accessible information can be seen in information disclosure requirements for toxic waste in the United States. Air pollution emissions were reduced by 35% in four years (Estes 1996a). This rate of progress could not have been achieved by regulation of emissions alone. Meeting regulatory requirements creates a burden for all but the largest corporations, as regulation is costly, intrusive and restrictive. Further, it is ultimately not sufficiently effective.

Business behaviour is best influenced not by changing rules governing what corporations may and may not do, but by changing rules governing the disclosure of information about what they do (Estes 1996a). Improved disclosure of CSR data and policies is required to convince the public that a company is responsive to their concerns about CSR (Alam 2000). A CSR report that is accessible to stakeholders is required, rather than multiple reports to a plethora of agencies. Making information more accessible to stakeholders through better disclosure of behaviour, rather than greater regulation of behaviour, is the key issue in corporate social reporting (Estes 1996a).

CSR and the Australian banking industry

There is no doubt that deregulation, globalisation and the introduction of new technology has improved efficiency and productivity in the Australian banking sector (O'Connell 1999); but bank management are now admitting that they have alienated many of their customers and other stakeholders in the process (Deegan 2000: 255).

The adherence of the banking sector to ethical principles came under fire in a recent court case. John Laws, a prominent Australian broadcaster, promoted the banks in a daily paid segment on his radio programme. The fact that Laws was paid to make these positive comments about banks was not disclosed at the time, creating concerns about a lack of transparency in these reports (Deegan 2000).

Evaluating the performance of banks as responsible corporate citizens and their success or otherwise in meeting the needs of all stakeholders is important, especially in Australia. Banks make up the largest industry sector on the Australian Stock Exchange (ASX). Approximately 18% of listed companies on the ASX are banks and there were seven other financial institutions in the top 20 companies in 1999. Virtually all Australians are stakeholders in banks in one way or another.

More households in Australia own shares (either directly or indirectly) than in any other country in the world (Eakin 2000). Many Australians became direct shareholders for the first time when the Commonwealth Bank was privatised with an initial public offering in 1991. Most Australian citizens are bank 'customers' either as depositors or borrowers, or both. Many will also be employees; the sector is one of the largest employers in Australia (although not as important as it used to be due to extensive redundancies in recent years). Outsourcing of services in banking, as in other industries, suggests there will also be a large body of contractors and consultants to the banking sector. Due to its sheer size alone, there will be many suppliers of goods and services to the banking sector. Further, the economy as a whole depends on the banking sector in its role as a conduit between borrowers and investors. All Australians stand to benefit from a socially responsible banking sector that reports CSR information in an open and honest way.

Reporting on environmental quality is an important aspect of the triple bottom line. Although banks have less direct impact on the natural environment than the chemical or mining industries, as large employers the sector consumes considerable amounts of natural resources and materials in terms of energy, water and paper. As such, they have the potential to guide other large employers in the efficient use of resources and take a leading role in environmental sustainability. In their role as intermediaries, they have developed efficient credit approval systems, capable of weighing and pricing risks, including environmental as well as financial risks. They can also play a role in promoting sustainability, through developing environmental or ethical investment funds (Jeucken and Bouma 1999). Unfortunately, there is evidence to suggest global financial institutions in the G100 are lagging the field in environmental reporting, as shown in Table 1. Only 7% of members of the financial services category provided environmental data in 1999. Australian banks are not represented in the G100.

	Financial services	Consoli-dated products	Electrical	Motor vehicles	Chemicals	Merchan-dising	Trading	Utilities	TOTAL
G100 firms in sector	30	4	16	12	11	8	8	11	100
Reporting firms	2	3	16	6	9	0	2	5	43
1999 firms reporting (%)	7	75	100	50	82	0	25	45	45
G100 firms in sector	21	6	13	14	19	11	11	11	106
Reporting firms	2	5	7	8	14	0	0	3	3
1998 firms reporting (%)	10	83	54	57	74	0	0	27	39

Table 1 GLOBAL ENVIRONMENTAL REPORTING DATA: 1998–1999

Source: KPMG 1999

Evidence is lacking on other aspects of CSR reporting for Australian banks. *The Good Reputation Index* is the first index to rank Australian companies by reputation. The top 100 companies were selected from *Business Review Weekly* (BRW) magazine's annual list of the top 1,000 companies. Whereas the BRW list of companies is ranked according to financial measures alone, the *Good Reputation Index* is based on a broader range of factors affecting reputation. The company with the best reputation is ranked number one. The reputation survey provides evidence of a growing *perception* that banks are concentrating on financial performance for shareholders, at the expense of other stakeholders. All banks included in the survey were ranked in the upper quartile of the top 100 companies based on financial performance, but ranked poorly on social indicators and ethics, as shown in Table 2.

These rankings were compiled from opinions of relevant stakeholders for each category, based on their perceptions of management practice. The reputation index results reported in Table 2 incorporate a financial and market position measure, which do not form part of an assessment of CSR practice. The remaining four measures—employee management, environmental, ethical and social impact—are considered to be related to CSR. It is interesting to note that the overall ranking of Australian banks in the top 100 companies index ranged from a high of 35 for Westpac Banking Corporation to a low of 70 for the Commonwealth Bank. The high overall ranking was due more to their financial performance—which ranged from second for the Commonwealth Bank to 13.5 for the other three banks—than to the CSR aspects of their performance. Changes in

	ANZ Banking Group (ANZ)	Commonwealth Bank of Australia (CBA)	National Australia Bank (NAB)	Westpac Banking Corporation (WBC)
Employee management rank	19	84	49	21
Environmental rank	94	65.5	82	19
Social impact rank	76.5	35.5	76.5	72
Ethical rank	55	92.5	55	100
Financial rank	13.5	2	13.5	13.5
Market position rank	38	72	73.5	46
Overall rank	46	70	69	35

Table 2 PERFORMANCE AND REPUTATION OF AUSTRALIAN BANKS: 2000

Source: Age/Sydney Morning Herald 2000: 3

computer technology have revolutionised the banking sector in Australia as in other parts of the world. These changes have allowed banks to outstrip other corporations in perceptions of financial performance for shareholders, but perceptions of Australian banks on general corporate citizenship criteria can be improved dramatically.

Tables 1 and 2 provide evidence of environmental reporting performance of non-Australian banks and stakeholder perceptions of CSR performance *per se* of Australian banks. As the focus of this study is on assessing the CSR reporting practices of Australian banks, a method other than a reputation survey is required. The next section considers data and methods.

Data and method

Davenport (2000) claims that there are three conditions that need to be addressed when operationalising corporate citizenship. First, there is the definition: what behaviours are indicative of 'good' corporate citizenship? Second, there is the problem of measurement: how to measure the quality of reported behaviour. Third, there is the question of accountability: who are the stakeholders to whom corporations are accountable. The premise adopted for this study is that the first criterion, i.e. behaviours indicative of 'good' corporate citizenship, are those identified by Glazebrook (1999); that is, social and environmental responsibility, governance, ethics, sponsorship, stakeholder relations and partnerships. The Sunshine Standards (see the Appendix) have been used to 'flesh out' these categories and this resulted in the following five criteria used in this study:

1. Corporate governance and ethics

2. Customer reporting

3. Employee reporting

4. Community/environmental reporting

5. Shareholder or stakeholder focus

Stakeholders to whom corporations are responsible—the third criterion—are assumed to be those identified in the Sunshine Standards. The second criterion identified by Davenport (2000), i.e. measurement method, is more problematic and requires further discussion.

Measurement method

Maignan and Ferrell (2000) identify and evaluate various methods for measuring CSR including the *Fortune* reputation survey, the Kinder, Lydenberg, Domini & Co. index (Simerly 1999) and the *Good Reputation Index* (2000) of Australian companies, mentioned above.

Reputation surveys measure perceptions of CSR performance, based on evaluations by stakeholders. It is not the focus in this study to measure CSR 'reputations' based on stakeholder perceptions. Rather, as previously stated, the aim is to interpret how open and honest management is in *reporting* CSR activities. To achieve this aim a different measurement method is required, one that concentrates on disclosure of CSR activities through the content in reports and/or other media.

Content analysis is a coding scheme, widely used to classify textual material, such as CSR reports. It can be applied to notes and non-quantitative data. Textual content is analysed by explicit rules called criteria of selection. The criteria must be established before the actual analysis of the data (Berg 1998). 'Quantification typically takes the form of either the number of documents containing a particular category of disclosure and/or the number of characters, words, sentences, pages, or proportion of pages devoted to different categories (or themes)' (Unerman 2000: 674).

Content analysis has several limitations (Gray *et al.* 1995; Milne and Adler 1999; Unerman 2000). Measuring volume, words and numbers alone is not sufficient. If pictures and graphics are ignored, the evaluation of the CSR report will be incomplete. Further, different treatment of pictures and typefaces when attempting to quantify CSR reports can lead to lack of consistency between studies. Numerical analysis provides a degree of objectivity, but accuracy might be achieved at the cost of a reduction in relevance of the study's results (Unerman 2000: 678). Despite the subjectivity of qualitative content analysis, it provides a system of criteria evaluation. As such, it overcomes many of the problems inherent in quantitative measures. Hence, qualitative content analysis was the method chosen for this study.

The qualitative information standards used to analyse and evaluate the quality of CSR reporting are drawn from work by Estes (1976, 1996a), Zadek *et al.* (1997), Ranganathan and Ditz (1997), Ranganathan (1999), Council for Economically Responsible Economies (CERES) (1999) and WBCSD (1999). Three primary criteria appear as a common theme when discussing qualitative standards in this context: relevance (to stakeholders), freedom from bias (by management) and understandability (to stakeholders).

Relevance

CSR reports meet the criterion of relevance if they are inclusive (cover all countries where the company is operating, for example), timely (a regular report and not just a knee-jerk reaction to bad news) and have substance. Measurement against industry benchmarks or peer companies adds substance, as does reporting of compliance with relevant international standards. Relevant international standards for CSR reports include standards for product quality (ISO 9000) environmental management (ISO 14000) and social accountability (SA 8000).[1] Reporting on dialogue with stakeholders is relevant, as are steps to implement the corporate code of conduct and corporate governance generally.

Freedom from bias

A CSR report meets the criterion of freedom from bias if it covers both good and bad news and is verified by an external party. Credibility and objectivity are the hallmarks of

---

1 Information on ISO 9000 and ISO 14000 is available from the International Organisation for Standardisation (www.iso.ch). SA 8000 is a standard on social accountability. Information is available from SGS International Certification Services (www.sgsgroup.com).

unbiased reports. Stakeholders are more likely to believe good news where any remaining problems are disclosed in an honest and open way (Elkington 1997). To be objective, a report must be verified by an independent third party, preferably a certified social auditor. An interesting aspect of external verification is that it is potentially culturally conditioned. Pruzan (1998) claims it is more important for US and UK companies than for Scandinavian companies because Scandinavian societies are characterised by smallness, homogeneity, less social conflict and very high levels of trust and transparency compared with other parts of the world. External verification is not seen as necessary to validate reports in these countries. However, even though there is little internal or external pressure for an audit to verify the 'truth and fairness' of Scandinavian corporate reports, the audit is seen as worthwhile. For example, critical analysis by an outside party may provide inspiration for improvement in practice. Australian society is closer to the US and UK than to Scandinavian countries in this respect, so external verification is important when applying the criterion of freedom from bias.

Understandability

Parsimony, achieved through the omission of trivial and excessive material, aids understandability, as does simple language. Reports are also more understandable if they are comparable, through time and between entities. Understandability is enhanced if companies quantify information where possible and report data in ratio form, rather than relying exclusively on text-based information. Graphics and tables, when used to summarise key points, can enhance understandability. Achieving a balance between parsimony and completeness is often difficult.

Reporting media

A further issue when evaluating CSR reporting practice is the source of information—the choice of documents to analyse. The use of websites to provide access to the annual report and other CSR information is growing in importance. Advantages of web-based CSR media include searchability attributes, increased depth and breadth of information, more timely updating of reports, ability to reach the young, reduced paper use and cost savings (GEMI 1998; SustainAbility/UNEP 1999). Many corporations provide access to special environmental reports on the web and the number disclosing social reports on their websites is growing.

Going beyond the annual report to other documents can provide a potentially rich data source for a case study of a single organisation, as shown in Unerman 2000, but presents difficulties for a cross-sectional study. Due to lack of conformity, navigating all aspects of corporate websites for CSR information is problematic. It is virtually impossible to identify all relevant communications, which makes a consistent analysis of cross-sectional data very difficult.

The majority of CSR accountability studies concentrate on analysis of corporate annual reports (Unerman 2000). Adams and Harte (1998) justify exclusive use of the annual report owing to its potential influence and the message communicated through what is *not* reported, as much as what is reported in the main form of corporate communication.

In Australia, banks, which are corporate entities, must produce an annual report. A common reporting medium is therefore available (Gray *et al.* 1995), so the annual report has been chosen as the primary reporting medium in this study. Where annual or special CSR reports are readily available through the corporate website, they have been used.

Sample selection

Although large in terms of value and overall impact on the Australian Stock Exchange (ASX), owing to mergers and acquisitions, the actual number of listed Australian banks is quite small. A structured, selective sample of Australian banks has been used in this study. All four major banks—ANZ Bank, Commonwealth Bank (CBA), National Australia Bank (NAB) and Westpac Banking Corporation (WBC)—have been included, because of their size and influence on the sector. Four regional banks, selected to allow representation from different states, have been added to give a total sample size of eight. Regional banks are: Bendigo Bank from Victoria, St George Bank from New South Wales, Bank of Queensland and Suncorp Metway. Data collected to evaluate CSR performance is taken from 1999 reports.

A global bank has also been included in the study in order to gauge how Australian banks perform in an international context. Credit Suisse has been selected for this purpose because of its inclusion in the Dow Jones Sustainability Index.[2]

The CSR content in annual and special reports for the selected sample of Australian banks is measured using the qualitative criteria of relevance, freedom from bias and understandability. What constitutes CSR and stakeholders is assumed to be as identified in the Sunshine Standards (see the Appendix). The cross-sectional results from content analysis of Australian banks operating in different regions and various sectors (large and small capitalisation stocks) are discussed in the next section.

Results and analysis

Reporting of Glazebrook's (1999) characteristics of 'good corporate citizenship' for Australian companies has been applied to Australian banks using three qualitative criteria: relevance, freedom from bias and understandability. Results for the 'big four' Australian banks are reported separately from those of the four representative regional banks.

Table 3 shows the results of qualitative content analysis for banks in the large capitalisation sector. Relevance is a function of substance. Unfortunately, lack of substance when reporting CSR activities is a feature of almost all aspects of the reports. Reporting on environmental quality is notable for its absence. This is consistent with stakeholder perceptions (Table 2) for CBA (65.5) NAB (82) and ANZ (94), but not WBC (19). Stakeholder perceptions of environmental concern by WBC are not supported by published information. Rankings depend on the performance of WBC relative to other corporations in the top 100 companies, so this could be suggestive of poor environmental practices by the other 80% of Australian companies. Alternatively, it could be because information on good environmental practice is not reported to stakeholders.

When the criterion of freedom from bias is applied to the major banks, ANZ is well ahead of the other banks. The result of a staff survey published in their annual report is an example of their willingness to report information in an unbiased way. Unfavourable as well as favourable performance against a benchmark is provided. ANZ's ranking for employee management is ahead of the other major banks, as shown in Table 2. In this case, the quality of the reported information seems to be consistent with stakeholder perceptions, although, again, reporting seems to be lagging behind perception in WBC's case.

Concision aids understandability in reports. It is easy to drown in too much information. ANZ's section dealing with customers, scores well on understandability owing to the concise reporting of outcomes and objectives by customer segment. Case studies have a role in reports and can add to understandability, although often at the expense of concision. The NAB scores well on coverage of community objectives and initiatives,

---

2 www.sustainability-index.com/index.html

REPORTING CRITERION / BANK	Corporate governance and ethics	Customer reporting	Employee reporting	Community/ environment reporting	Shareholder or stakeholder focus	Ranking and additional comments
ANZ Banking Group (ANZ)	Appears to be narrowly based code of conduct for executives in report	Concise reporting of outcomes and objectives by customer segment	Results of staff survey published—performance against other companies reported	Support for staff volunteerism Financial assistance—financial and recipient	Stakeholders identified as shareholders, staff, customers and community	▶ Broader view of stakeholders than other big four banks; employees appear to be included as major stakeholder ▶ Best for employee reporting (although room for improvement) ▶ Unbiased reporting of results from staff satisfaction survey—willing to report against peers, even when unfavourable ▶ Objectives for 2000 provided, but could be difficult to measure ▶ Nothing on environmental performance
National Australia Bank (NAB)	Reference to code of conduct with 'strict ethical guidelines' issued to all staff	Case studies by customer segment	Nothing of substance reported on employees	Key objective to be a 'socially responsible organisation'—community case studies	Stakeholder focus in vision and value statements includes customers and communities	▶ Good coverage of community objectives and initiatives ▶ Code of conduct appears to go beyond mere regulatory compliance ▶ Very poor coverage of employee information, not included as stakeholders ▶ Nothing on environmental performance
Westpac Banking Corporation (WBC)	Reference to being a 'good corporate citizen'	Case studies by customer segment	Nothing of substance reported on employees	Limited to reporting sponsorship of athletes	'Stronger customer and community focus as key to shareholder value'	▶ Ahead of other banks in ethical investment initiatives (but not covered in annual report of WBC) ▶ Code of conduct appears to go beyond mere regulatory compliance ▶ Very poor coverage of employee information, not included as stakeholders ▶ Nothing on environmental performance
Commonwealth Bank of Australia (CBA)	Reference to statement of professional practice including EEO	Case studies on youth, individuals, families, rural, business and institutional customers	Nothing of substance reported on employees	Nothing of substance reported on community partnerships	Focus on customers and shareholders in report but reference to staff in value statement	▶ Social responsibility is implied in the focus on a broader shareholder base—including young people and rural customers ▶ Very poor coverage of employee information ▶ Lack of coverage of philanthropic activities, employee volunteerism or community partnerships ▶ Nothing on environmental performance

Table 3 CSR REPORTING: BIG FOUR AUSTRALIAN BANKS

whereas CBA has focused on young people and rural customers in its annual report. NAB and WBC also provided illustrative case studies by customer segment, but these lacked the substance evident in CBA's report.

When the criteria of relevance, freedom from bias and understandability are applied to the 'big four' Australian banks, ANZ is ranked first. Although, in common with other banks, there is nothing on environmental performance, it includes more information relevant to CSR than the other banks. Although arguably deficient, ANZ's focus on employees in particular as major stakeholders places it well ahead of other banks in CSR reporting.

Apart from a similar lack of attention to environmental performance, the CSR performance of Australia's regional banks is more positive in comparison with the 'big four' banks. Bendigo Bank is ranked first in the small market capitalisation sector and overall. Its report provides substantial CSR information of relevance to customers, employees and the community generally. As with WBC, it has ethical investing alternatives available for customers, including a Community Aid Abroad initiative. Its social reporting appears to be more consistent with CSR objectives than all the other banks in that it focuses on responsible corporate citizenship through partnerships with the community rather than philanthropy.

All of the regional banks score well on understandability as applied to the customer reporting indicator. The Bank of Queensland, for example, scores well on relevance and understandability with its report on a 'free mornings' initiative, when customers can make withdrawals without transaction fees. Suncorp Metway provides case studies on various types of customer group and St George reports on the link between customers and the creation of shareholder wealth (Table 4).

Evidence of freedom from bias, however, is hard to find in the regional banks. All banks, apart from ANZ on a single employee indicator, did not report hard evidence of both good and bad performance against benchmarks.

CSR reporting lags behind environmental reporting globally (CERES 2000). As shown in Table 1, financial institutions generally are lagging the field in reporting environmental performance. Australian banks are notable, however, for their almost total lack of reporting on the environment. Table 5, analysing the CSR performance of Credit Suisse, a global bank included in the Dow Jones Sustainability Index, illustrates how far Australian banks need to go to achieve best practice in environmental reporting. CSR reporting for Credit Suisse is done on a voluntary basis, as is the case for Australian banks, although it needs to be acknowledged that the cultural 'climate' and public pressures may be different for Credit Suisse than for Australian banks.

With some exceptions, publicly available information on environmental impact and sustainability initiatives is increasing across a broad range of industries and throughout many regions in the world, but financial institutions generally are lagging behind, as are Australian banks. An evaluation of the current state of play suggests that the Australian banking industry is still in an embryonic phase when it comes to reporting most social and environmental issues.

Conclusions

Good corporate citizenship requires transparency when reporting on CSR activities. A commitment to a triple-bottom-line reporting system is required: a system that, in addition to *financial* information, values *social* responsibility and *environmental* sustainability, recognising that open and honest reporting of these attributes is as essential as open and honest reporting of *financial* performance. The objective of this study was to

REPORTING CRITERION / BANK	Corporate governance and ethics	Customer reporting	Employee reporting	Community/environment reporting	Shareholder or stakeholder focus	Ranking and additional comments
Bendigo Bank	More substance to ethics and code of conduct than other regional banks	Clear focus on customers. Case study and figures on growth in customers and lending approvals.	Reporting of long-service leave awards with specific staff identified. Comparison of staff numbers over two years	Community partnerships—focus on citizenship rather than charity. Case studies.	Clear stakeholder focus, customers and community	▲ Best regional bank for report CSR reporting ▲ Ethical Investment Trust, Community Aid Abroad Initiative, established in 1992—'socially and environmentally beneficial' investments—all proceeds distributed to CAA ▲ Emphasis on descriptive reporting of CSR activities; greater emphasis on CSR facts and figures would provide a more balanced view of activities ▲ Nothing on environmental performance
Suncorp-Metway	Code of ethics is narrowly based—little beyond insider trading.	Case studies on various types of customer group	Reporting of desire to avoid reducing staff levels and redundancies	Reporting of staff volunteerism and community initiatives	Stakeholder focus, reference to customers, employees, shareholders	▲ Runner-up regional bank ▲ Philanthropic rather than community/partnership approach, but employee engagement in community fund-raising activities represents a move towards a partnership approach ▲ Emphasis on descriptive reporting of CSR activities ▲ Nothing on environmental performance
Bank of Queensland	Narrowly based reference to ethical and legal compliance manual only	'Three Free Mornings' initiative: withdrawals without transaction fee for customers	Reference to staff survey. Facts and figures not reported. Increase in staff numbers reported.	Lacks substance. 'Continued commitment to commercial, community and philanthropic initiatives'.	Objectives re contribution to Queensland growth, linked prosperity. Shareholder focus in report.	▲ Report geared towards shareholders ▲ Little of substance for other stakeholders ▲ 'Three Free Mornings' is a good social initiative that could assist customers with lower balances—'feature no other bank offers' deserves more attention in report ▲ Reporting of results from staff survey would enhance report ▲ Little of substance on CSR in report ▲ Nothing on environmental performance
St George Bank	Almost exclusively based on avoidance of insider trading	Core strategies focused on customer link to creation of shareholder value	Reporting of maternity leave and high rating by female staff. Star awards.	Financial assistance in dollars provided through St George foundation	'Working with other stakeholders ⇒ maximise shareholder value'	▲ Focus on shareholder value as ultimate aim—staff meet needs of customers; customers provide value for shareholders ▲ Reporting of results from staff and customer surveys would enhance report ▲ Little of substance on CSR in report ▲ Nothing on environmental performance

Table 4 CSR REPORTING: AUSTRALIA'S REGIONAL BANKS

REPORTING CRITERION / BANK	Corporate governance and ethics	Customer reporting	Employee reporting	Community/environment reporting	Shareholder or stakeholder focus	Ranking and additional comments
Credit Suisse, one of the leading sustainability companies in banking sector in Dow Jones Sustainability Index	New group-wide code of conduct introduced in 2000 with 12 core values and guiding principles Supplements compliance manuals, guidelines and policies including environmental policy	Little of substance on performance in meeting customer objectives in annual report	Reference to: ▼ Job creation ▼ Graduate employment ▼ Training programmes ▼ Equal opportunity but lacking in substance	Detailed report on energy, material and resource savings Brief overview of charitable commitments and sponsorship	Vision and values statement not provided Annual report focuses clearly on shareholders Separate report on environmental performance Lack of focus on other stakeholders	▼ Comprehensive coverage of environmental performance, including ISO 14001 compliance ▼ Unbiased report on environmental performance, including weaknesses as well as strengths ▼ Facts and figures provided on environmental performance, as well as policies, objectives and case studies, bi-annual report from 1995/96 improving through time ▼ Represented in 10 portfolios run by ecological/ethical funds ▼ Segment report on CSFB 'group in society' but social reporting is well behind environmental reporting

Table 5 CSR REPORTING: GLOBAL BENCHMARK BANK

evaluate whether the reports of Australian banks are relevant, free from bias and understandable in the way they report CSR activities.

Problems with defining and identifying what constitutes 'good' corporate citizenship have been addressed through reliance on work by Glazebrook (1999) and Estes (1996a, 1999). It could be argued, however, that the indicators selected for this study are not the only areas that are indicative of good corporate citizenship or exclusively demand reporting.

There are problems with measuring the quality of CSR information and the choice of documents used to assess the quality of reported CSR information. The lack of easily accessible data, difficulties of data capture and differences in research approach are endemic in CSR research (Gray *et al.* 1995) and this study is no exception. The method of analysis overcomes the problems of attempting to quantify CSR information. The researchers recognise that it relies on subjective assessment in linking the criteria—relevance, freedom from bias and understandability—to the categories presented in Tables 3, 4 and 5 and how these criteria are used to evaluate the quality of CSR information.

Leaving these limitations aside, the question of whether Australian bank management reports CSR activities in an open and honest way is not clear-cut. There is evidence to suggest that Australian banks perform well on the single bottom line of financial performance. If we take a more balanced approach, one that considers the triple bottom line of environmental and social performance as well as financial performance, Australian bank reports leave a lot to be desired. There is much to be done if Australian banks are to achieve best practice in CSR reporting.

On a more optimistic note, dialogues between business and non-business stakeholders are on the increase in Australia as elsewhere. The banking industry is a late starter in comparison with corporations in the resources sector, for example, but there is a growing recognition in Australian banks that business is part of the solution to creating a more stable, healthy and prosperous world. Response to a global shift in social and ethical values has been an increased interest in CSR reporting by Australian banks.

There is some evidence in this study of a move towards more customer- (and in some cases community-) focused reports, for example, with most of the banks providing case study information. Moreover, the banks appear to be committed to a stakeholder rather than just a shareholder focus, but there is little evidence in reports of a strong commitment to implementation of practices commensurate with a broader stakeholder focus. Statements appearing under 'corporate governance and ethics', for example, are lacking in substance and appear to focus on compliance. Put more simply, Australian banks appear to be recognising the need to move beyond a blinkered shareholder approach to a more broadly based stakeholder approach, but this recognition has not been followed with action as yet. It must be remembered that concentration on a particular stakeholder group or groups does not necessarily mean that a company has a 'stakeholder focus' (Goodpaster 1991). It may indicate that, at any point in time, one particular group of stakeholders is considered more important to a company than another.

The Bendigo Bank provides the best stakeholder-focused report. There is evidence to suggest that it has gone beyond mere lip-service to a broad stakeholder focus and there appears to be more substance to its code of conduct than is the case with other regional and the 'big four' banks. Generally, most of the CSR content from the banking sector appears to be long on rhetoric and short on substance. As in other parts of the world, CSR reporting is at an embryonic stage in Australian banks.

Directions for future research

Previous studies have relied primarily on quantitative rather than qualitative measurement techniques. As explained above, standards such as relevance, freedom from bias and understandability have been applied so that quality as well as quantity is assessed when evaluating CSR information. The reporting media have been limited to the annual report and any special CSR reports available in hard copy or on websites. Difficulties in web navigation led to this constraint. If all relevant information is provided in a concise way in the annual report only, is this better than more extensive information spread out over several reports and or sources, or hidden deep within a web sub-sub-site? Future research could consider whether the source of information and accessibility to that information is a factor to be considered when evaluating the quality of CSR reports.

This study has been limited to the banking sector and is therefore unlikely to be indicative of CSR reporting in Australia generally. A comparative study of the banking industry with other sectors in Australia would shed further light on the state of play of CSR reporting in Australia.

A global bank, Credit Suisse, was included in the sample to provide an international context. The inclusion of Credit Suisse in the Dow Jones Sustainability Index means that it represents best practice for environmental reporting, but not necessarily for social reporting. Future research should include other global banks that provide examples of best practice in social reporting in different cultural contexts.

There are several stages involved in the transition from a company that ignores CSR or simply pays lip-service to it, to a fully committed company. There is evidence to suggest that Australian banks recognise the need to report triple-bottom-line activities, but statistics indicating such activities are rarely reported in practice at this stage. In a fully committed company, CSR reporting will have evolved through time to a stage where it addresses a broad range of social issues, such as those outlined in the Sunshine Standards. Relevant issues will be reported in a manner that is free from bias and is understandable. Companies learn from industry best practice. A comparative study such as this provides guidance to banks in their evolutionary path to better CSR reporting practice.

References

Adams, C. (2000) 'Ethical Reporting: Past and Future', *Management Accounting* 78.2: 48-50.

Adams, C., and G. Harte (1998) 'The Changing Portrayal of the Employment of Women in British Banks' and Retail Companies' Corporate Annual Reports', *Accounting, Organizations and Society* 23.8: 781-812.

Age/Sydney Morning Herald (2000) 'The Good Reputation Index', an *Age/Sydney Morning Herald* Special, 30 October 2000.

Alam, N. (2000) 'Company Reporting on Social Issues: The Case for Greater Disclosure', *Corporate Governance International* 3.1: 10-22.

Altman, B.W., and D. Vidaver-Cohen (2000) 'A Framework for Understanding Corporate Citizenship' (introduction to the special edition, 'Corporate Citizenship for the New Millennium'), *Business and Society Review* 105.1 (Spring 2000) 1-7.

Berg, B.L. (1998) *Qualitative Research Methods for the Social Sciences* (Boston, MA: Allyn & Bacon).

Birch, D. (2000) *Corporate Social Responsibility: Towards Sustainable Capitalism* (Working Paper; Melbourne: Corporate Citizenship Research Unit, Deakin University).

Birch, D., and M. Glazebrook (2000) *Stakeholder Relations: Corporate and Community: Perspectives from Australia* (Working Paper; Melbourne: Corporate Citizenship Research Unit, Deakin University).

Buchholz, R. (1995) *Business Environment and Public Policy: Implications for Management* (Englewood Cliffs, NJ: Prentice–Hall, 5th edn).

CERES Global Reporting Initiative (1999) 'Towards a Common Framework for Corporate Sustainability Reporting', *International Symposium, Imperial College, London, 4–5 March 1999* (updated 13/01/99), www.ad.ic.uk/cpd/unep.html.

CERES Global Reporting Initiative (2000) 'Sustainability Reporting Guidelines on Economic, Environmental and Social Performance', June 2000 (updated 31 December 2000), http://ceres.org/reporting/globalreporting.html.

Davenport, K. (2000) 'Corporate Citizenship: A Stakeholder Approach for Defining Corporate Social Performance and Identifying Measures for Assessing It', *Business and Society* 39.2: 210-19.

Deegan, C. (2000) *Financial Accounting Theory* (Roseville, Australia: McGraw–Hill).

Eakin, J. (2000) 'Individuals steal march in direct share ownership', *The Business Age*, 19 August 2000: 2.

Elkington, J. (1997) *Cannibals with Forks: The Triple Bottom Line of 21st Century Business* (Oxford, UK: Capstone Publishing).

Estes, R. (1976) 'Standards for Corporate Social Reporting', *Management Accounting* 19.2: 26.

Estes, R. (1996a) *Tyranny of the Bottom Line: Why Corporations Make Good People Do Bad Things* (San Francisco: Berrett–Koehler).

Estes, R. (1996b) 'A New Scorekeeping System', *Business Ethics* (special report no. 1), December 1996: 3-7.

Estes, R. (1999) 'The Sunshine Standards and the Stakeholder Alliance: A Win³ Program for Business, Stakeholders and Society', keynote address to *Conference on Leadership Loyalty and Lies: Business Ethics for the New Millennium*, Victoria University, Melbourne, 19 February 1999.

Francis, R. (2000) *Ethics and Corporate Governance: An Australian Handbook* (Sydney: University of New South Wales Press and Australian Society of CPAs).

Freeman, R.E. (1984) *Strategic Management: A Stakeholder Approach* (Boston, MA: Pitman).

Friedman, M. (1962) *Capitalism and Freedom* (Chicago: University of Chicago Press).

GEMI (Global Environmental Management Initiative) (1998) 'Environmental Reporting and Public Availability of Corporate Environmental Data', in *Communications in the Environment Health and Safety Value Equation Conference, March 1998* (updated May 1998, cited 10 February 2000), www.enviroreporting.com.

Gibson, K., and G. O'Donovan (2000) 'Environmental Disclosures in Australia: A Longitudinal Study', in *6th Interdisciplinary Environmental Association Conference*, Montreal, Canada, 21–24 July 2000.

Glazebrook, M. (1999) *Corporate Citizenship and Action Research: An Australian Perspective* (Paris: International Association of Business and Society Proceedings): 120-25.

Goodpaster, K.E. (1991) 'Business Ethics and Stakeholder Analysis', *Business Ethics Quarterly* 1.1: 53-73.

Gray, R., R. Kouhy and S. Lavers (1995) 'Methodological Themes: Constructing a Database of Social and Environmental Reporting by UK Companies', *Accounting, Auditing and Accountability Journal* 8.2: 78-101.

Hooghiemstra, R. (2000) 'Corporate Communication and Impression Management: New Perspectives Why Companies Engage in Corporate Social Reporting', *Journal of Business Ethics* 27.1–2: 55-68.

Husted, B., and D. Allen (2000) 'Is it Ethical to Use Ethics as Strategy?', *Journal of Business Ethics* 27: 21-31.

Jeucken, M., and J. Bouma (1999) 'The Changing Environment of Banks', *Greener Management International* 27 (Autumn 1999): 21-35.

KPMG (1999) *International Survey of Environmental Reporting* (Amsterdam: KPMG).

Maignan, I., and O. Ferrell (2000) 'Measuring Corporate Citizenship in Two Countries: The Case of the United States and France', *Journal of Business Ethics* 23.3: 283-97.

Milne, M., and R. Adler (1999) 'Exploring the Reliability of Social and Environmental Disclosures Content Analysis', *Accounting, Auditing and Accountability Journal* 12.2: 237-56.

O'Connell, B. (1999) 'Baptism by Fire: How Adversity Primed Australia's Banking Industry for a Brave New Era', *Journal of Banking and Financial Services*, December 1999: 12-28.

O'Donovan, G. (1999) 'Managing Legitimacy through Increased Corporate Reporting: An Exploratory Study', *Interdisciplinary Environmental Review* 1.1: 63-99.

Pruzan, P. (1998) 'From Control to Value Based Management and Accountability', *Journal of Business Ethics* 17.13: 1379-94.

Ranganathan, J. (1999) *Sustainability Rulers: Measuring Corporate Environmental and Social Performance* (Washington, DC: World Resources Institute, updated 24 January 2001, www.ig.org/wri/meb.pdf/jnet.pdf).

Ranganathan, J., and D. Ditz (1997) *Measuring Up: Towards a Common Framework for Tracking Corporate Environmental Reporting* (Washington, DC: World Resources Institute, www.igc.org/writ/meb/measure/mup-toc.html).

Shiraz, A. (1998) 'Social Reporting: Nice Idea But', *Australian CPA* 68.10: 58-59.

Simerly, R. (1999) 'Measuring Corporate Social Performance: An Assessment of Techniques', *International Journal of Management* 16.2: 253-57.

Simerly, R. (2000) 'A Theoretical Examination of the Relationship between Chief Executive Officers and Corporate Social Performance', *International Journal of Management* 17.2: 218-23.

Solomon, R. (1992) *Ethics and Excellence* (New York: Oxford University Press).

Spence, L., and J. Lozano (2000) 'Communicating about Ethics with Small Firms: Experiences from the UK and Spain', *Journal of Business Ethics* 27: 43-53.

Sweeney, M., and R. Estes (2000) 'Corporate Social Reporting and the Sunshine Standards: Is there light at the end of the tunnel?', *Conference on Ethical Governance and Management: Costs and Benefits*, Business Ethics Research Unit, Victoria University, Melbourne, 31 March 2000.

SustainAbility/UNEP (United Nations Environment Programme) (1999) *The Internet Reporting Report* ('Engaging Stakeholders' programme; London: SustainAbility, April 1999, www.sustainability.co.uk/publications/engaging/internet-report.asp).

Unerman, J. (2000) 'Methodological Issues: Reflections on Quantification in Corporate Social Reporting Content Analysis', *Accounting, Auditing and Accountability Journal* 13.3: 667-80.

Vidaver-Cohen, D., and B. Altman (2000) 'Concluding Remarks, Corporate Citizenship in the New Millennium: Foundation for an Architecture of Excellence', *Business and Society Review* 105.1 (Spring 2000): 145-68.

Watts, P., and L. Holme (1999) *Meeting Changing Expectations: Corporate Social Responsibility* (Geneva: World Business Council for Sustainable Development).

WBCSD (World Business Council for Sustainable Development) (1998) 'Corporate Social Responsibility: A Dialogue on Dilemmas, Challenges, Risk and Opportunities', Leeuwenhorst Congress Centre, Langelaan 3, Noordwijkerhout, Netherlands, 6–8 September 1998, www.wbcsd-org.ae.psiweb.com. csr.csr2.pdf .

WBCSD (World Business Council for Sustainable Development) (1999) *Social and Environmental Ledgers* (www.wbcsd.ch/csr/csr10.pdf , updated 13 December 2000).

Zadek, S., P. Pruzan and R. Evans (eds.) (1997) *Building Corporate AccountAbility: Emerging Practices in Social and Ethical Accounting, Auditing and Reporting* (London: Earthscan Publications).

Appendix: stakeholder alliance Sunshine Standards

EXAMPLES OF INFORMATION THAT CORPORATE STAKEHOLDERS MAY NEED FOR RATIONAL ECONOMIC DECISION-MAKING

For customers

▶ Product liability, injury and wrongful death claims that have been brought against the company

▶ The corporation's record of indictments and citations for regulatory violations

▶ Recall data for each product model including when and why recalled, with evidence of whether the problem has been corrected in the present unit

▶ Product contents classified to reflect current dietary and safety concerns

▶ Biodegradability of packaging

▶ Automotive air pollution emissions ratings, by specific model

For workers

▶ The company's history on lay-offs and shutdowns, over time and across facilities, along with a statement of its lay-off policy

▶ Information about the risks on each job: exposure to chemicals, smoke, fumes, toxic substances, fibres, dust; hazards associated with the use of tools and equipment; the danger of repetition of movement; radiation levels from computer equipment, laser printers, television and microwaves

▶ Data on past illnesses, injuries, medical complaints and other work-related health problems classified by job, department, date and nature of the problem

▶ Gender and race information on: (1) compensation levels, (2) new hires during the year, (3)

promotions, and (4) number in position at year-end, broken down by such categories as (a) top executives, (b) other top management, (c) second-level management, (d) middle management, (e) line, (f) clerical and (g) custodial.

▶ Employee turnover data by department, level, gender, race and age category

▶ Data on promotions from within as opposed to external hires

▶ Full information concerning employee pension programmes, including changes in market value of investments and the extent to which past and current benefit liabilities are funded.

For communities

▶ An enumeration of legal actions brought against the corporation for the past five years, from whatever source and in whatever jurisdiction, describing the nature of the claim or charge, parties involved and status or disposition

▶ Corporate history on tax exemptions, forgiveness, or deferrals, zoning changes previously sought, and other favours granted to the corporation, along with verifiable data on jobs created in response to such benefits

▶ Estimates of the quantities of waste and sewage that will be generated, with separate estimates for amounts and types of waste accompanying product use

▶ Taxes paid to all jurisdictions: property, corporate income, unemployment, workers' compensation, social security, severance (wellhead, natural resource extraction), sales

▶ Radioactive, toxic, hazardous and dangerous materials used or stored at sites within the community or transported, by or on behalf of the corporation, through or within one mile of the corporate limits of the community. Title III of the Federal Superfund Amendments and Reauthorisation Act of 1986, often called the 'Community Right-to-Know Act,' requires such disclosure, but both communities and the EPA report that they still cannot obtain the data they need.

▶ Information on plant construction including data on presence of asbestos, structural defects, ground preparation and prior use if known. For example: was the facility built on a waste dump?

▶ The proportion of materials purchased from local sources, especially in communities that have given corporations large tax breaks

▶ Air and water emissions, by specified category and quantity (some data is presently available, but is not adequate for community policy decisions)

▶ Company unemployment compensation rating and record (since this provides insight into the company's record of employment stability)

▶ Political contributions broken down by candidate, party or issue (such as a referendum or charter ordinance). Data should be spelled out for any corporate-controlled political action committees (PACs) as well as for corporate officers and managers.

For society at large

▶ Amount and content of trade with nations that is officially discouraged as a matter of national policy

▶ Amount of foreign exchange generated and used, to permit an assessment of the extent to which the corporation is contributing, favourably or unfavourably, to the balance of trade

▶ Major government contracts, by nature and dollar amount

▶ Penalties above a specified minimum imposed by regulatory agencies over the past five years

▶ Federal taxes actually paid, and the amount by which US taxes were reduced each year by foreign tax credits

Source: R. Estes, The Stakeholder Alliance, 1735 S Street, NW, Washington, DC, 20009-6117, USA

Corporate Barbarism to Corporate Citizenship

A Psycho-philosophical Inquiry

Shitangshu Chakraborty

Indian Institute of Management, Calcutta, India

This paper is a brief attempt to discuss corporate citizenship, not in terms of codes or systems or legislation, but in terms of some deeper psycho-philosophical insights into human existence—both individual and collective. It offers a critique of economics and economic growth, as demonstrated through their harmful social-psychological and ecological effects, from the long-term, macro viewpoint. Two major Hindu-Vedantic psychological theories of human personality have been briefly explained and used to probe corporate incivility or barbarism in the era of 'capinomics' (capitalist economics). The duty-focused, common good-oriented concept of *lokasangraha* has been introduced to provide a deeper foundation for corporate citizenship. This should inspire the ascent of corporate character to the plane of corporate trusteeship. Corporations may then emerge as agents of sane 'spirinomics' (spiritualised economics), instead of reckless capinomics.

- Corporate citizenship
- Psycho-philosophy
- Capinomics
- Corporate trusteeship
- Spirinomics

Professor S.K. Chakraborty has been teaching and researching at The Indian Institute of Management, Calcutta, since 1971 in the areas of finance and control and human values, ethics and Indian ethos. He has published widely and runs an annual residential workshop on human values and ethics for managers and executives at the Institute. He edits *The Journal of Human Values* and is presently convenor of the Management Centre for Human Values in the Institute.

✉ Indian Institute of Management, PO Box 16757 Alipore PO, Calcutta, India 700027

🖥 sitangsu@iimcal.ac.in

JCC 4 *Winter 2001*

109

But if Science has prepared us for an age of wider and deeper culture . . . it has encouraged more or less indirectly both by its attitude to life and its discoveries another kind of barbarism—for it can be called by no other name—that of the industrial, the commercial, the economic age. This economic barbarism is essentially that of the vital man (Aurobindo 1972: 72).

Barbarism: the psychological root

ECONOMICS GIVES NO QUARTER TO DEPTH PSYCHOLOGY. PSYCHOLOGY RECOILS from philosophy. Commerce has nothing to do with sociology. Technology has no truck with ethics. History shuns spirituality. Management and literature stand poles apart. Due to such learned incapacity or reluctance among various professional disciplines for respectful intercourse, the fashionable phrase 'holistic thinking' has become a mere platitude. So I open this paper with a quote from Sri Aurobindo who, having attained holistic realisation, transcends all kinds of disparate speculation and narrow expertise.[1]

The word 'barbarism' commonly suggests the absence of decorum, honour, gentlemanliness, refinement, nobility and the like. In contrast, it stands for coarseness, brutality, vulgarity, etc. While science and, today, technology, may have caused the demise of the purely **body**-centred primitive barbarian, they have bred and pampered the modern barbarian who is centred in the **vital**. Aurobindo's theory of psychological evolution of the human being can be summed up as a hierarchy of four levels: body–vital–mind–spirit. The **vital** level of consciousness is thus explained by him (Aurobindo, 1977: 290):

> it is a realm of desires, not only sexual or physical desires, but desires for power, activity, ambition, pride . . . in its crude form this vital urge appears as lust, desire for possession, for money, for enjoyment of all kinds.

Now, the key difference between the primitive and the modern barbarian is the almost unlimited extension of the domain of the vital, achieved and executed with great cleverness, by the latter. The primitive barbarian was more innocent; the modern is more scheming.

The **mind** (thinking, reasoning, etc.) is in principle a higher and superior level of human consciousness. It is expected to master and lead the vital being in us. But the reality is too often the opposite: the master becomes the servant, the leader the led. In the absence of systematic psychological education and training, the **mental** being functions like an 'ineffectual angel beating its luminous wings in the void in vain' (Arnold 1960: 147).[2] Consequently, the mind usually becomes an accomplice of the barbaric vital, yet denies that this is so through the art of rationalisation.

Economic barbarism, then, is that reductionist consequence of modern civilisation that invariably and unquestionably reduces every thought and act of ours to money terms. Money is now the end, the measure of everything, not a means any more. The elevation of the corporation as the commander-in-chief in the trumpet-march of economic barbarism can be traced to *The Wealth of Nations* (Smith 1991). It is significant evidence of the supremacy of the vitalistic barbarian in the **homo-economicus** that the

---

1 Sri Aurobindo (1872–1950) studied classics and history at Cambridge for 14 years (1889–93). After playing a leading role in the Indian freedom movement, he went to Pondicherry for the exclusive pursuit of the Divine, the Transcendental, the Supramental. But he kept regular contact with the happenings in the world. His collected writings in English constitute 30 volumes. The opening quote is from an essay he wrote some time during 1916–18.

2 The essay on Shelley from which this line is quoted was written by Mathew Arnold in 1888 in the journal *The Nineteenth Century*.

same author's earlier work, *A Theory of The Moral Sentiments* (Smith 1976), has had practically no influence on the formation of corporate character. Thus, as the corporate world has already proved, the mind has lost to the vital. If the corporate entity has an independent legal status of its own, one should then be able to speak with equal validity about 'corporate character'. Corporate civility or corporate citizenship can flow only from the source: corporate character. This suggests that due importance be given to human values within the corporate deep structure.

Sometime in May/June 1929, during an address in Japan, Rabindranath Tagore[3] (1996: 623-25) observed:

> Through this *creative limitation* which is our personality, we receive, we give, we express. Our *highest social training* is to make our property the *richest expression* of the *best in us* . . . [emphasis added].

> . . . with what is called material progress, property has become *intensely individualistic*; the method of gaining it has become a matter of science and *not of social ethics* [emphasis added].

> Thus, society, which should be our field of cooperation, has become that of *competition*, in which, through its tyrannical standard of respectability, all the members are goading one another to *spoil themselves* to the uttermost limit [emphasis added].

Although Tagore did not use the word 'barbarism' to characterise these tendencies, the import of what he says is unmistakable.

Aurobindo and Tagore have been quoted above at some length because we shall need such far-sighted insights to interpret current corporate incivility, in India as well as elsewhere. Corporations are the fountainheads through which the vast subterranean lava of economic barbarism gushes up to the surface. Of course, positive examples, though fewer, will also follow.

Citizenship: the philosophical impulse

Let us now take a quick look at citizenship from a philosophical perspective, the previous perspective being psychological. From the 1946 UN Declaration of Universal Human Rights to the Indian Constitution of 1950, and to the latest human rights organisations of many shades, 'rights' is the right mantra to utter and use. Duty is a dirty word. The word 'citizen' or 'citizenship' is normally used in academic literature in the political sense. It comprises objective, legalised rights and entitlements of persons as members or residents of a state or nation. But they are all minimal conditions for protection against unjust exclusion or victimisation. They 'give' some legitimacies to a person residing in some part of the word. But with these 'givens' what is the citizen expected to 'give' in turn? For only then we can step beyond the limited field of 'objective' citizenship into the great arena of full-blooded 'subjective' citizenship, however complex and subtle it might be. The only reasonable approach here seems to be the philosophy of 'human duties'.

I feel that the preceding argument is equally tenable when the focus is shifted from the individual citizen to the corporate citizen. Let us recall that initially the word 'admin-istration' was considered adequate to cover the conduct of affairs both in government and business. In the second stage the word 'management' gained currency with refer-

---

3 Rabindranath Tagore (1861–1941) was the most prominent Indian figure in literature and art in contemporary times. He was a poet-philosopher–painter–musician–teacher all rolled into one. He was awarded India's first Nobel Prize in 1913. His *Collected Works* add up to more than 30 volumes. Like Aurobindo, Tagore also travelled, lived and studied in the West for long periods.

ence to business only. Somewhere along the line governments too (in India at least) thought 'administration' was not smart enough for them. They too began to embrace the word 'management'—at least to sound modern. In the latest phase, in the last ten years or so, 'governance' has replaced 'management' in the business lexicon. Are corporate entities becoming so unmanageable that now they have to be 'governed'? The Greek root for governance is *gubernau*, which means 'to discipline, to rule'! Reviewing the last three decades of the 20th century, I submit the hypothesis that this nemesis of corporate existence is rooted in the lop-sided rights-oriented philosophy of our times, at the expense of a duties-oriented ethos. The philosophy of free-market economics has twisted the meaning of freedom to one of unbridled exercise of only such rights as the business élite define for themselves. Witness the latest manoeuvres of the world's biggest pharmaceutical firms against the Indian firm CIPLA, which can supply cheap remedies for AIDS to South Africa. Once again a clear proof of the dictatorship of the vital.

When we study the ancient, sacred literature of sustainable civilisations such as India, China and others, we invariably discover that, from the God-to-the-Sage-to-the-King-to-the-Laity, the entire chain of exchange process is projected as an unending cycle of mutual duties only. The word 'rights' or its equivalent does not figure anywhere in the great Indian epics of the *Ramayana* or the *Mahabharata*. The known and unknown seers and compilers of these works were indeed much wiser than we regard ourselves to be. With penetrating insight these sacred social legislators saw clearly this truth: *duties are the cause; rights are the effect.* Each person, each agent, each organisation doing its appropriate appointed duty in a rightful manner (**dharma**) automatically causes the satisfaction of rights for relevant constituencies. For example, the teacher doing his or her duty to prepare implies meeting the students' right to learn. The bureaucrat doing his or her duty of selfless service results in the preservation of a certain right of a citizen. The head of a nation doing his or her duty of leading a transparent and noble life honours the citizens' right to have a worthy role model. And so it goes on.

There is yet another important philosophical corollary about why duties need to be prioritised over rights. Rights always emphasise one side of the equation: from other(s) unto me. But duties concentrate on the opposite: from me unto other(s). I believe that this angle to the theme of citizenship should be given adequate space and time in our educational processes for society and culture-building activities within organisations— from the founders and CEOs downwards. The old, unfashionable elixir of duties, pure and simple, must seep once more into all the exchanges within society, and those between human society and the earth-system that holds it. Such a revival could be the real antidote to the 'self-destructive basis of self-interest' (Saul 1997: 36).

We know that work and work ethic are central to the practice of citizenship. Lasch has traced the changing meaning of work ethic during three centuries of American history: work as a means for self-improvement first, self-preservation next, and self-advancement thereafter. The current view of work is overwhelmingly one of self-advancement, which we often see as degenerating into self-interest and self-aggrandisement (Lasch 1991: 52-57). It is not unreasonable to infer that this sort of transition has been positively correlated with the apotheosis of rights. When corporate bodies, too, replicate this model of individual character, and inevitably so, eventually duty-centred citizenship gets pushed to the back seat, and rights-oriented barbarism comes to the front.

As we discuss citizenship from the viewpoint of rights versus duties, it is also useful to reflect a little on the intriguing shift of idiom from 'corporate social responsibility' to 'corporate citizenship'. I can only speculate on a possible reason for this displacement of 'responsibility' by 'citizenship': perhaps the word responsibility is too categorical in its duty-centred connotation. This might be making both individuals and corporations feel uncomfortably restricted in the exercise of freedom on their own terms. Citizenship, on the other hand, being a politically rooted rights-oriented word, leaves our minds light and easy. It allows enormous scope for flexibility in the realm of 'ought' and 'should'—which in any case is a rather marginal notion in the domain of pragmatic *realpolitik*.

Capinomics, competition and corporate citizenship

In this section I will cite a number of examples in our times which have bordered on barbarism. Some of the agents may have made amends after wide public exposure. But the fact is that such atrocious corporate behaviour has occurred at one time or another.

Capitalist economics (capinomics) revolves around the hub of free-market competition. Andrew Carnegie, in a vigorous **vitalistic** defence of this central tenet, asserted that the law of competition is best for the human race because it ensures the survival of the fittest. For its sake the resultant great environmental inequality and concentration of business must be accepted and welcomed. They are beneficial as well as essential. Intense individualism embedded in competition is a key force (Carnegie 1889: 654). This sort of simplistic, linear abstraction fails to reckon with the reality of human (corporate) character or human (corporate) psychology. Tagore's principle of 'creative limitation' in personality development is simply ruled out. History proves continuously this truth about human conduct: competition can bring out the worst as much as the best of the individual (or corporate entity). When the worst is excited, we shall have corporate barbarism. If the best is aroused, we shall tend to witness corporate citizenship. It is the general impression that, these days, instances of corporate barbarism far outnumber those of corporate citizenship. Why is it so?

In the previous section attention was drawn to a major *philosophical* principle which occupies the heart of contemporary upbringing and education: deification of rights-consciousness and devaluation of duty-consciousness. At the beginning of the paper I offered a key *psychological* insight which could help us to understand the growth of barbarism and decline of citizenship in individual or corporate existence. This psychological insight shall be pursued a little more in this section in the context of competition.

In Nature's evolutionary course for the human race the 'vital being' has experienced a much longer infra-rational phase compared with the rather recent emergence of the rational-mental stage. The crude instinctive vital being in the human constitution 'persists even when it is trained by the growing application to it of enlightening reason' (Aurobindo 1972: 154). Consequently:

> The modern attempt of reason in the form of a broad and thorough rational, utilitarian, and efficient instruction and organization of man and his life is not succeeding . . . for all its insistent but always illusory promise of more perfect results in the future (Aurobindo 1972: 155).

This accurate but humbling insight into human psychology, along the evolutionary time-scale, should add some measure of modesty and sobriety to our discussions on and prescriptions for corporate citizenship, too. For corporations are no more than larger collectives of the still predominantly vitalistic man coated with a thin veneer of reason. While this raw and strong vital being continues to be our effective inner ruler, then competition is more likely to show us its barbaric face than its benign face. The vital being enjoys grabbing and devouring. It easily forgets, even wants to forget, that Carnegie had also recommended simple and unostentatious living for the wealthy who should hold wealth as a trust for society (Carnegie 1889: 661). Let us now offer some examples of capinomics in practice.

One area of corporate behaviour where barbarism is rather conspicuous is that of compensation packages for CEOs and top management. Singer, for instance, presents quite a range of data to reveal this state of affairs. Thus, by 1991, the average pay of a

CEO in the US had risen to 160 times that of a worker (Singer 1989: 31). The comparable Japanese and German ratios were way below this level. Singer comments a little later: 'Greed at the top is one side of a society that appears to be losing any sense of a common good' (1989: 32). And, for me, citizenship, based on duties, is surely all about common good. India's corporate world seems to trust the American approach more than the Japanese approach.

In an interesting and provocative book, based on ample field study in the US, Blumberg has shown us numerous pictures of the 'predatory' face of American business (Blumberg 1989). For instance, he laments the irony that, in a much-vaunted knowledge society, widespread public ignorance is a rich mine for experts to exploit. He has it right when he says: 'public ignorance gives the expert leverage to maintain and enhance his earnings, power and status' (Blumberg 1989: 75). Quoting from a survey report by another organisation, Blumberg informs us that, in 1984, 70% of the respondents agreed that American business and industry 'are far too often not honest with the public', and 68% said that American business and industry 'has lost sight of human values in the interest of profit' (Blumberg 1989: 201).

Some time in the early 1980s, one among the fastest-growing private-sector businesses in India had produced a perfect example of the ugly face of competition, spurred by the raw vitalistic craving for growth in no time. As reported in newspapers, a neighbouring dignified and adequately profitable government enterprise had been manufacturing and selling a certain chemical which required cryogenic tankers for transport. The enterprise itself did not own any such tankers. So it relied on two private parties who hired out these carriers. This was a long-standing arrangement. Now, the private enterprise also began to manufacture this speciality chemical, and it too did not possess cryogenic tankers. So, as part of an aggressive product launch strategy, and to teach the public enterprise a lesson in professional management, this private-sector company simply hired out for the next three months, at exorbitant rates, the entire fleet of such tankers from both the parties. However, its own needs were actually a small fraction of the total fleet strength of the two parties. The public enterprise was stunned by this move, and could do nothing. Its production and distribution of the particular product simply came to a grinding halt.

The infamous conduct of the giant British Airways against the puny Virgin Atlantic is yet another sordid instance of barbaric vitalism getting the better of civilised business behaviour. Here was sharkish crookedness at its worst in an attempt to snuff out a small competitor (Kitson and Campbell 1996: 27-37).

Burrow and Helyar, in a large and meticulously documented book, have vividly described how 'barbarians at the gate' assailed the corporate world to conquer the now-famous corporate Godhead: shareholder wealth maximisation (Burrow and Helyar 1990: 28, 171). The massive narrative provides numerous accounts of unbridled greed and ambition of deal-driven, yield-driven, nomadic non-company men whose avowed aim was to serve company investors. Of course, this tended to serve themselves handsomely as well. One of the word-pictures about what corporate citizenship should never be like emerges from them (Burrow and Helyar 1990: 177):

> Once Kohlberg got his hands on a company, he ruthlessly cut costs and sold unwanted business, freeing up every extra dollar to pay debts. In most cases he gave management stock incentives, which he found did wonders for their ability to run the business more efficiently. When he was done, the leaner, meaner result was usually worth more than when he bought it. In their most basic guise, LBOs have worked the same way ever since.

As the wisdom goes, however, out of every evil cometh some good. In the months following the RJR Nabisco buy-out, many on Wall Street had begun to sense a slow surge of civility in the takeover world, almost as a backlash, as it were, against greed and hubris (Burrow and Helyar 1990: 623).

Subhash Chandra, who wanted to emulate Rupert Murdoch in the Indian media business, provides another stark example of greed unlimited. Obsessed with the single goal of higher and ever higher stock prices, he is reported to have made 81 big 'announcements' during the year 2000 each one of which had pushed up Zee TV's stock price. Each Rs. 10 share peaked to Rs. 1,630 in February 2000. But, then, most of the announcements were phoney, and nemesis struck the company when its stock price touched the all-time low of Rs. 260 in November 2000 (Rajsekhar *et al.* 2000: 21). Chandra also nursed the ambition of competing with the giant Reliance group in the fibre-optics business. And holding as he did 66% of the equity of Zee TV, soaring stock prices meant booming personal wealth for him, too.

Justice Jackson chastised the business behaviour of Microsoft CEO, Bill Gates, as one that had systematically 'attempted to obliterate by unfair means any competition', as being veritably 'untrustworthy', as that of an abusive monopolist—all of which required the framing of 'interim conduct rules'.[4]

The Shell Group inserted a two-page advertisement in *The Economist*[5] proclaiming that 'human rights' was a business priority for them. It is 'the heart of our business', the copy announces. Seeing this, a visiting scholar from a New Zealand university to the Management Centre for Human Values told us how well known it was that this very group had been vilified for its association with the military regime in Nigeria.

One of the most gripping legal battles about corporate citizenship was fought in the UK a few years ago. Two UK citizens circulated a factsheet attacking the fast-food giant McDonald's for its use of advertising, its promotion of an unhealthy diet, its exploitation of staff and the environmental damage it caused (Vidal 1997: 136-38).

Concealed behind the dazzling mask of being the number one company in the US for several years, there seems to exist a dismal corporate citizenship record at GE. 'Criminality within GE hit its apex at the very time it was most profit-driven and treating its employees with the most egregious disregard. Certainly greed has also contributed to lawlessness' (O'Boyle 1999: 14). From the tradition of paternalism GE turned to cannibalism. 'Loyalty' became a bad word and was deleted from GE idiom. 'Purposeful insecurity' took its place (O'Boyle 1999: 15).

The few examples recounted above show how contradictory the raw vital being of corporate personality is today in terms of what can be generally expected of corporate citizenship.

By showing linkages between professionalised competitive sports, student responses and business conduct, the fearful face of free-market competition seems to be beginning to resemble a state where one 'could conceive of no competition that did not result in someone's annihilation' (Lasch 1991: 117). As to why and how self-centredness among university students is causing 'survivalism [to take] the place of heroism as the admired quality' is explained in Bloom (1988: 84). So, competitiveness and barbaric survivalism have become familiar bedfellows. Honour is a human value that does not fit the vitalistic psychology of success orientation. Yet citizenship is perhaps all about being honourable.

Korten draws a perceptive distinction between capitalism and competition. Offering some latest data and examples, he concludes: 'Competition is key to the self-organizing dynamics of a market economy. In contrast, capitalism loves monopoly with a passion equalled only by its abhorrence of the competition that limits its ability to extract monopoly profits' (Korten 1999: 43).

Speaking of competition in a psychological vein, Singer likens the process to that of 'the labours of Sysiphus—a sentence to never-ending labour without a goal. It is an addiction . . .' (Singer 1989: 244). The same grim warning about insatiability for more and

---

4 *The Economist*, 10 June 2000: 67.
5 23 September 2000: 94-95.

ever more was portrayed in the Indian epic *Mahabharata* through the poignant story of King Yayati, which we have called the 'Yayati syndrome' (Chakraborty 1991: 270-303).

In other words, competition is usually not the most healthy propeller of good citizenship. Many corporations and their founders and CEOs do become billionaires, apparently through competitive battles. They may then give away a few millions for charitable and other public welfare activities, possibly as some kind of atonement for their predatory competitive tactics. But this cannot be a worthy recipe for ideal corporate citizenship. The means and motives are its most significant ingredients.

Swami Vivekananda (1863–1902), India's first modern exponent of Vedantic-Hindu psycho-philosophy in the West, had these words about competition for an American audience in the 1890s (Vivekananda 1959: V, 278), barely a few years after Carnegie's eulogy for it:

> These competitions and struggles and evils that we see . . . are in the way . . . The more I study history, the more I find that idea to be wrong . . . I find now that every war has thrown back human progress by fifty years instead of hurrying it forwards. The day will come when men will study history from a different light and find that *competition is neither the cause nor the effect*, simply a thing on the way, *not necessary to evolution at all* [emphasis added].

In other words, the competitive spirit to overstep or outstrip or excel the other(s) in terms of any measurable criterion makes the competitor psychologically precarious and aggressive. The ego-centred vital being then wallows in a state of war-mindedness. Therefore, honourable corporate (or individual) citizenship becomes the first casualty whenever the vital being fears any erosion of its pre-eminence. The preceding examples all lend sufficient credence to this thesis.

It is safer by far, therefore, to proceed to build a theory and framework of citizenship—corporate or individual—on a radically different and positive philosophy about human personality: wholeness and perfection are already 'involved' as the core of the human frame. The task of managing society and its institutions is to allow this 'involved' perfection to evolve and manifest itself in our external existence. This is what Vivekananda's words emphasise. And this is the biblical wisdom too: the kingdom of heaven is within. The pioneering cybernetician, Stafford Beer, almost a century after Vivekananda, has discerned this fundamental wisdom in the gnostic writings, too, suppressed for a long time by the established church. Further, he attributes the origin of such 'living within' psychological training in gnostic literature to Eastern and Yogic influences (Beer 1994: 386-87). The competitive spirit in capinomics, in contrast, is exclusively a 'living without' existential formula.

Corporate citizenship and *lokasangraha*

The most syncretic of all psycho-socio-philosophical texts in the Vedanta-Hindu tradition is the *Bhagwadgita*. It comprises 700 verses, delivered as wisdom counsels to a worthy army general by his wise charioteer in the centre of a battlefield. This battlefield could be treated as an allegory for the endless clashes between right and wrong in human life. The key concept of **lokasangraha** occurs in verse III-20 of the *Gita*. Rendered into English it reads thus: 'It was even by works that Janaka (the King) and the rest attained to perfection. Thou shouldst do works regarding also the *holding together of the peoples*.'

'Holding together of the peoples'—this is the essence of *lokasangraha*. As Sri Aurobindo explains at length, the striving for 'common good' embedded in *lokasangraha* certainly embraces the higher ego-reducing ideals of social service, humanitarianism, cosmopolitanism and collectivism. All these take us a long way towards *charismatic* character and constructive citizenship. But he is careful enough to point out, though some readers may not consider it as quite relevant in the limited context of this paper, that the ultimate import of *lokasangraha* is works done through spiritual identity with Godhead, stripped completely of one's (individual or corporate) vitalistic ego (Aurobindo 1977: 54).

In India, several public enterprises established by the government in all the core sectors of the economy since the 1950s have been, in our view, very apt examples of *lokasangraha*, worthy corporate citizenship. They set up massive industrial complexes in the most inaccessible areas of the country. Around the plants sprung up townships, schools, hospitals, playgrounds, clubhouses, places of worship, market complexes and so on. Beautification and enhancement of the environment by these enterprises have also been impressive. When massive natural disasters such as earthquakes and floods have struck, they have always responded with handsome monetary and technical support for the hapless victims and affected localities. A wide range of common goods indeed.

It is quite another tragedy that, due to the growth of heavily politicised and rights-oriented trade unionism among all categories of employees, buttressed by job security, the work ethic within the workplace declined rapidly. Much of the enterprise-related financial losses in these public enterprises could be traced to such irresponsible trade unionism. Another major reason for poor bottom-line results in many enterprises was the deliberately fashioned low pricing policy for their outputs—since they were the basic industries whose outputs would be the inputs for a much larger range of secondary industries—mainly in the private sector. Besides, the bureaucrats in government also tended, by and large, to treat these enterprises as arenas for exercising their power-lust. This was yet another damper to the effectiveness of a fundamentally correct approach towards corporate citizenship in a developing country such as India.

But, since the dawn of the Thatcherite era of bottom-line capinomics with privatisation as the sole engine of prosperity, the entire public sector has become an object of derision, only to be cursed and buried. And, of course, with its gradual burial, *lokasangraha* or corporate citizenship, as a moral philosophy for industry, has also become an antediluvian notion. Instead of 'holding together of the peoples', the pressure tactics from international financial agencies, executed through astronomically expensive restructuring reports from big foreign consulting firms, are forcing these enterprises to slash manpower with stunning speed. They are also withdrawing from spending on common goods. All this is being done under duress and by dangling the futile hope of increased international competitiveness for Indian products. Also, it should be noted, such manpower flexibility measures are being forced on a society that is characterised by 'high population–low employment' as a grim reality.

In private-sector industry, too, a few glorious Indian examples of quiet, humble and sustained corporate citizenship may be cited. The two most prominent ones are the business houses of Tatas and Godrej's. They both possess more than a century of admirable track record in this regard. It must be pointed out that these industrial enterprises were created during British rule in India. The mainspring behind them was neither maximisation of shareholder value, high corporate rank-order position, nor topslot personal wealth ranking. Their empowerment sprang from ardent patriotism— to prove the point to their politico-economic masters that Indian enterprises, too, could match their British counterparts in quality, price and range. Hence, *lokasangraha*—that is, corporate nobility towards society as a whole—was a spontaneous expression of their feeling of duty towards it. It was not sleek public relations masquerading as corporate citizenship. A recent book about Godrej's makes the following pertinent observations:

> responsibility for the development and security of our vast and complex country cannot be left to the government alone. A variety of resources and talents have to be harnessed

to promote the development of diverse dimensions of Indian society that are way beyond the goodwill and even the capacity of democratic governments (Karanjia 1997: 311).

The house of Tatas has pursued corporate citizenship on a far more comprehensive scale than any other Indian business group. Thus:

> Between themselves the Tata Trusts have created an infrastructure for the balanced development of the nation in science, technology and the social sciences. They have launched pace-setting institutions that have given India its first institute for social sciences, its first cancer hospital and research centre, and its first institute for fundamental research in physics and mathematics that gave India a head-on start in its atomic energy programme (Lala 1992: 161).

It should be emphasised that the above acts for the sake of common good (*lokasangraha*) by both the industrial houses were not meant to assuage a pricking conscience. The spending came from straightforward profits earned through honourable competition with imported British products (e.g. steel, chemicals, textiles, office and domestic security products).

Another very large and old industrial house of Birlas, and a modest new one of Bhilwaras, also deserve mention. Though their public image does not appear to be as impeccable as that of the two cited above, they too have demonstrated positively what corporate citizenship can achieve. The father figure of the house of Birlas once (1935) wrote a letter to his son which contained advice of the following nature (Chakraborty 1999: 211):

> Never use wealth for luxury and cheap pleasure . . . Wealth is never eternal; therefore so long as it lasts use it for serving others.

> Do leave this advice for your children: if they lead a life of comfort and luxury they would be committing sin and destroying our business activities. You must not bequeath wealth to such spoilt brats.

> Remember always that you hold wealth on behalf of the common citizens. You cannot use it for selfish ends.

It is obvious that the above guidelines are way above cosmetic calls for corporate citizenship. The Bhilwaras (launched in 1962) have also promoted, through various trusts, a number of schools, publication of serious books, donations to charitable and spiritual organisations and the like. Corporate barbarism was explained earlier in terms of acts of aggression and winning at any cost. This means, psychologically, that the 'vital being' gains the upper hand in the make-up of the modern corporate personality. What, then, is the alternative psychological principle that could sustain the kind of corporate citizenship exemplified above?

Among the few plausible answers that may be possible, the one we suggest here is this: knowingly or unknowingly, the founding fathers and captains of these industrial houses were acting mainly from the level of their 'psychic being',[6] supported by the psychological energy-force of 'illumination' (**sattwa guna**).[7] As an approximation we might say that the 'psychic' is the spirit-core in our chain of being or hierarchy of personality. But, unfortunately, it remains concealed, cornered by the barbaric 'vital' layer of our being. The ruthless acquisitiveness of the vital being is fuelled by the

---

6 A concise psychological interpretation of the 'psychic being' is given here from Sri Aurobindo: 'The psychic is the inmost being of all; a perception of truth which is inherent in the deepest substance of the consciousness, a sense of the good, true and beautiful is its privilege' (Dalal 1989: 18).

7 **Sattwa guna**, or the illumining psychological energy-force in the human being, is that power or mode of cosmic nature that confers insight and bestows enlightened understanding, followed by harmonising and equilibrating knowledge for decision-making (Aurobindo 1977: 205-208).

psychological energy-force of 'blind dynamism' (**rajo guna**).[8] Springing from the 'psychic' being of corporate personality, created by the founders whose own psychic being was somehow not overshadowed by the vital, these enterprises exhibited the illuminated, unpretentious dynamism of *sattwa guna*. The unseeing dynamism of *rajo guna*, expressible through the unruly 'vital' being, was not allowed to make a mockery of *lokasangraha* or corporate citizenship.

Corporate citizenship, economic growth and cosmic decline

Let us revisit the economic barbarism of capinomics in this section in order to visualise, to a degree, the future prospects for corporate citizenship. Of course, this will be a purely subjective view of the author.

In early September 2000 newspapers across the world flashed this piece of information: that both NASA and the World Meteorological Organisation had measured a hole 11 million square miles in size in the ozone cap over Antarctica. This area is four times as large as that of the US. Is there a fact more telling than this to size up the awesome nature of cumulative aggregate corporate barbarism during the last three centuries of economic development pursued through science, technology and industry?

Yet fanatical espousal of economic growth remains as strong as ever. Just preceding the November 2000 UN summit on global warming in The Hague, *The Economist* editorial did somehow manage to say: 'The time has come to accept that global warming is a credible enough threat to require a public-policy response.'[9] Yet it insists that economic growth must be sustained, that the world cannot be stopped, that there are risks of slowing economic growth. All this is advocated because only this way, we are advised, can the resources be generated to meet the costs of global cooling. Strange logic indeed. The very kind of economic growth that has caused global warming over the past is now being championed as the global coolant for the future! The devil is the angel too! Refusal to learn is among the greatest virtues (?) of our times.

In more detailed coverage on the subject, the same issue of *The Economist* uses an interesting linguistic ploy—probably to divert our attention from the cosmic dimension of economic and corporate barbarism. It poses a question: 'Does mankind deserve the blame?'[10] It suits us perfectly well to substitute 'economic growth' and 'corporation' for 'mankind'. Answering this question, the article refers to a NASA research study and informs us:.

> Under normal circumstances the earth releases heat at the same rate at which it absorbs energy from the sun. But the researchers conclude that man's actions since 1850 have upset this balance. Man-made GHGs now cause a forcing of more than two watts per square metre—the equivalent of increasing the sun's brightness by around 1%.[11]

And, as the article goes on to inform, American business in particular has been vocal in insisting that any cuts in greenhouse gas emissions (the Kyoto target being a modest lowering by 5% by 2008–12 from the levels of 1990) would come only at 'tremendous economic cost' (2000b: 100). The following words from David Korten make sober reading in this context (Korten 1999: 186):

---

8 **Rajo guna**, or the kinetic psychological energy-force in the human being, is that power or mode of Nature that spurs lust for action, along with all the low-grade vitalistic emotions such as envy, treachery, arrogance and vanity, duly followed by disruptive actions (Aurobindo 1977: 206).

9 18 November 2000: 19.

10 18 November 2000: 98.

11 *Ibid.*

> The courts have moved persistently . . . in the direction of expanding corporate rights and increasing the autonomy of corporate management . . . corporations now enjoy unlimited life, virtual freedom of movement anywhere on the globe, control of the mass media, the ability to amass legions of lawyers and public-relations specialists in support of their cause, and freedom from liability for the misdeeds of wholly owned subsidiaries.

This, then, is the grim scenario for future growth-driven corporate citizenship against the cosmic backdrop of global warming (and much else). And didn't we also say in an earlier section that the philosophy of rights is anti-citizenship?

At the earthly level, too, even as we emphasise the theme of *lokasangraha*, 'the holding together of peoples', as the keynote of corporate citizenship, the role of multinational corporations (MNCs) or transnational corporations (TNCs) cannot be ignored. Since the days of the East India company, corporate colonialism, through royal charters, has been a common method of several European countries. During the last 20 years, this brand of colonialism has been scaling new heights of sophistication. As one commentator observes: 'In the South today transnational corporations continue to operate as colonial machines by producing and reproducing inequality and dependency' (Clarke 1999: 158). Institutions such as the World Bank, the International Monetary Fund, the Organisation for Economic Co-operation and Development and the World Trade Organisation are together ensuring that TNCs have easy rights to cheap raw materials and labour, have power to redirect internal production priorities, and endlessly repatriate profits without local government interference in Southern countries (Clarke 1999: 158). Even in the Northern countries, where the Keynesian social welfare economics model was jettisoned in favour of the Thatcherite–Reaganite model of the 1980s, governments are being forced to provide security for investors, not for the citizens (Clarke 1999: 160).

Way back in 1958, John Kenneth Galbraith had already warned that it was the value of Social Darwinism that had substantially 'broadened the claim for the market', narrowing thereby the scope for social measures to help or protect the less fortunate people from 'the hazards of economic life' (Galbraith 1958: 60). And we read, almost 40 years later, having witnessed soaring economic growth, this rueful observation from Saul: 'In a corporatist system there is never any money for the public good because the society is reduced to the sum of the interests. It is therefore limited to measurable self-interest' (Saul 1997: 37). All this, then, constitutes the matrix of our discourse today about corporate citizenship, on both the terrestrial and the cosmic planes.

Corporate citizenship: grounding in SPIRINOMICS

We are inclined to turn here to two Indian minds who possessed a rare blend of both insight and foresight about the human condition. They are Rabindranath Tagore, mentioned earlier, and Mahatma Gandhi (1869–1948). In the lecture quoted in the first section Tagore was saying that the rich men of property in India used to do all kinds of public works for common good, *lokasangraha*, 'through a spontaneous adjustment of mutual obligations'. This was possible because the Indian social system had set strict limits to the right of self-indulgence so that the 'surplus wealth easily followed the channel of social responsibility' (Tagore 1996: 623). In an earlier (1920) address in Gujarat, which is a relatively prosperous state in western India, Tagore referred to the Hindu goddess, Laxmi. She symbolised not only wealth but also sacredness, goodness and beauty—a kind of ideal plenitude. Later he took his Indian audience to task for banishing Laxmi for money only, 'which we not only pursue, but bend our knees to it'. He went on to add:

> such a state has come to pass because with the help of science, the possibility of profit has suddenly become immoderate. The whole of human society . . . has felt the gravita-

tional pull of a giant planet of greed with its concentric rings of innumerable satellites. It has carried to our society a distinct deviation from its moral orbit (Tagore 1996: 404).

Eighty years since Tagore thundered thus, the psychological-moral temper of humanity is today many times more mammonistic and demoralised. Our thoughts on corporate citizenship for the next 80 years need honest cognisance of the real character of its deep stratum.

Tagore's reflections and warnings about wealth and welfare, money and greed, voiced from his deep poetic intuition, were given a more concrete shape with a distinct name by Gandhi: trusteeship. Without mincing words, resonating perfectly with the archetypal drift of the Indian mind, he dashes off like this (Gandhi 1969: 365):

> Everything belonged to God and was from God. Therefore wealth was for the people as a whole, not for a particular individual. When an individual had more than his proportionate portion he became *trustee* of that portion for God's people.

It is possible that, to the dry rationalist, or the logical intellectual, Gandhi's words might sound like utopian trash. But what Gandhi may have expected, at least from some of us, is that we learn that, unless all human endeavour has some sacred and higher reference point than its self-centred mundane obsessions, its sense of social responsibility, *lokasangraha*, will lack the power of inspired conviction. Even if the corporate citizenship movement starts off well grounded in intellectual-normative roots, like many other similar movements it could soon degenerate into much calculative posturing or cosmetic window-dressing in practice. To escape such ignominy Gandhi declared: 'I am inviting those people who consider themselves as owners to act as *trustees* i.e., *owners not in their own right, but owners in the right of those whom they have exploited*' (Gandhi 1969: 366; emphasis added). In other words, Gandhi is prepared to give no more quarter to the man of business than that of an obliged intermediary between God and the common citizen. Tagore's goddess Laxmi is the mythical, benign guide for the secular man of commerce for his sacred journeys between these two poles.

Having been allowed to use 'Goddess' and 'God' through Tagore and Gandhi in their thesis of welfare and trusteeship, we might as well be permitted to use the same word through another Indian contemporary of Tagore and Gandhi. It is Swami Vivekananda who made these remarkably prescient observations in the 1890s (Vivekananda 1959: I, 425): 'The difference between God and the devil is in nothing except in unselfishness and selfishness . . . Apply the same idea to the modern world: *excess of knowledge and power, without holiness, makes human beings devils*' [emphasis added].

Here is one more grim reminder to us about the inherent difficulty at the starting point itself for the ascent of corporate citizenship to its potential summit.

To return to the psychological framework outlined briefly in some of the earlier sections, an outline of a theory for corporate citizenship seems to emerge like this:

> *Lokasangraha* or *common good* being its keynote, the leaders/owners/ founders/members of corporates need to relearn about themselves cognitively, and then pursue experiential assimilation, in terms of the duty-oriented *psychic, and self-transcending* being, supported by the conscious nurturing of the psychological energy-force of *equilibrating illumination* or *sattwa guna*.

Clearly, this is a long-gestation investment of intense conviction, crystallised in the unbroken crucible of wisdom experience of ancient seers and modern sages. Can we muster the courage?

Towards the close of this paper we may strike a tragi-comic note. After furnishing us with an overview of genetics, robotics and nanotechnology, Bill Joy informs us, quite joylessly, that, by being downloaded into our technology, through self-multiplying intelligent robots and other glorious things round the corner by 2030, either human beings will not exist in the sense that we understand now, or the human species itself could be extinct (Joy 2000: 240). Wonderful! With no human citizens around, who the hell needs corporate citizenship! What's all this fuss and noise about? For whom? Corporates: please march merrily and rapidly towards 2030, dumping aside the dirt-heap of sterile citizens.

This paper began by referring to Sri Aurobindo's 'economic barbarism'. I return at the end to him again, who, after all, had some words of hope, too, coupled with deep caution (Aurobindo 1992: 73):

> in a commercial age with its ideal, vulgar and barbarous, of success, vitalistic satisfaction, productiveness and possession the soul of man may linger a while for certain gains and experiences, *but cannot permanently rest.* If it persisted too long, life would become clogged and perish of its own plethora or burst in its straining to a gross expansion. Like the too massive Titan it will collapse by its own mass, *mole ruet sua.*

A momentous choice for the corporate citizenship movement for the furtherance of *lokasangraha*[12] (common good, for holding together of peoples), then, is: should it meekly submit to the sci-tech juggernaut and be a minister to its biddings with some cosmetic facelift here and there? Or, should its psychology and philosophy be underpinned by the firm and clear conviction that sci-tech, and material manipulation and comforts through it, are engagements subordinate to the furtherance of the true goal of the human race: unfoldment and manifestation of the already-perfect spirit in man? It is time we pay respectful attention to the realised wisdom of the likes of Aurobindo who belong to our own era and have seen through it from inside out.[13] They induce the hope that gradually capinomics will allow itself to be transformed into spirinomics—economics subordinated to the Spirit—furthering its cause within both the individual and the corporation. Then, the aim of spirinomics

> would be not to create a huge engine of production, whether of the competitive or the cooperative kind, but to give to all . . . the joy of work according to their own nature, free leisure to grow inwardly, as well as a simply rich and beautiful life (Aurobindo 1972: 241).

Of course, stupendously patient conviction is required to steer the course of corporate citizenship towards such a destiny. The stubborn rejection of the 'moral sentiment' (ethics) by establishment capinomics is unlikely to mellow at an early date. For even those who have genuine concerns for environment and ecology are ridiculed by capinomics as eco-fundamentalists.[14]

References

Arnold, M. (1960) *Essays in Criticism* (ed. S.R. Littlewood; London: Macmillan, 2nd series).
Aurobindo, Sri (1972) *The Human Cycle* (Pondicherry, India: Sri Aurobindo Ashram).
Aurobindo, Sri (1977) *The Message of the Gita* (Pondicherry, India: Sri Aurobindo Ashram).
Beer, S. (1994) *How Many Grapes Went into the Wine* (ed. R. Harnden and A. Leonard; Chichester, UK: John Wiley).
Bloom, A. (1988) *The Closing of the American Mind* (New York: Simon & Schuster).
Blumberg, P. (1989) *The Predatory Society* (New York: Oxford University Press).
Burrow, B., and J. Helyar (1990) *Barbarians at the Gate* (London: Arrow Books).
Carnegie, A. (1889) 'Wealth', *North American Review* 148.391: 653-62.
Chakraborty, S.K. (1991) *Management by Values* (New Delhi: Oxford University Press): 270-99.
Chakraborty, S.K. (1999) *Wisdom Leadership* (New Delhi: Wheeler Publishing).

12 Hazel Henderson, writing about the growing importance of civic society to withstand the assaults of information bombardment, seems to have unwittingly echoed this very imperative: 'this is forcing us to "go inside ourselves" and ask some pretty basic questions' (Henderson 1999: 56).
13 The Japanese **kyosei** concept seems to have similar implications to those of *lokasangraha*.
14 *The Economist*, 2 December 2000: 96-97.

Clarke, T. (1999) 'Twilight of the Corporation', *The Ecologist* 29.3: 158-62.

Dalal, A.S. (1989) *Living Within* (Pondicherry, India: Sri Aurobindo Ashram).

Galbraith, J.K. (1958) *The Affluent Society* (Harmondsworth, UK: Penguin).

Gandhi, M.K. (1969) *Selected Works. Vol. VI* (ed. S. Naryan; Ahmedabad, India: Navjivan Trust).

Henderson, H. (1999) *Beyond Globalization* (Hartford, CT: Kumarian Press).

Joy, B. (2000) 'Why the future does not need us', *Wired*, April 2000: 238-47.

Karanjia, B.K. (1997) *Godrej: A Hundred Years. Vol II* (New Delhi: Viking).

Kitson, A., and R. Campbell (1996) *The Ethical Organization* (London: Macmillan).

Korten, D.C. (1999) *The Post-Corporate World* (San Francisco: Berrett–Koehler; West Hartford, CT: Kumarian Press).

Lala, R.M. (1992) *The Creation of Wealth* (Bombay: IBH Publishing).

Lasch, C. (1991) *The Culture of Narcissism: American Life in an Age of Diminishing Expectations* (New York: W.W. Norton).

O'Boyle, T.F. (1999) 'Perfect at Any Cost', *Business Ethics*, March/April 1999.

Rajsekhar, M., M. Anand and A. Balkrishna (2000) 'Planning a Comeback', *Business World* 20.30: 20-26.

Singer, P. (1989) *How are we to live?* (Sydney: Text Publishing).

Smith, A. (1976) *The Theory of Moral Sentiments* (Oxford, UK: Oxford University Press).

Smith, A. (1991) *The Wealth of Nations* (New York: Random House).

Saul, J.R. (1997) *The Unconscious Civilization* (Ringwood, Victoria, Australia: Penguin).

Tagore, R. (1996) *The English Writings of Rabindranath Tagore. Vol. III* (ed. S.K. Das; New Delhi: Sahitya Academy).

Vidal, J. (1997) *McLibel* (London: Macmillan): 136-38.

Vivekananda, Swami (1959a) *Collected Works. Vols. I and V* (Calcutta: Advaita Ashrama).

THE JOURNAL OF
CORPORATE
CITIZENSHIP

SUBSCRIBE NOW

And save up to 30% on your subscription!

▶ **2-YEAR OFFER**
subscription rate (8 issues)

SAVE 30%

Organisations: £210.00/$350.00
(Usual price £300.00/$500.00)

Individuals (must be paid from private funds): £105.00/$175.00
(Usual price £150.00/$250.00)

▶ **1-YEAR OFFER**
subscription rate (4 issues)

SAVE 15%

Organisations: £127.50/$212.50
(Usual price £150.00/$250.00)

Individuals (must be paid from private funds): £63.75/$106.25
(Usual price £75.00/$125.00)

• *Offers are not available through subscription agencies.*

Orders should be sent to: Greenleaf Publishing, Aizlewood Business Centre,
Aizlewood's Mill, Nursery Street, Sheffield S3 8GG, UK
Tel: +44 114 282 3475   Fax: +44 114 282 3476
E-mail: sales@greenleaf-publishing.com

Or order from our website: www.greenleaf-publishing.com

Diary of Events

October 2001–June 2002

A selective listing of key conferences, seminars and exhibitions in the field of corporate responsibility

15–16 October 2001   London, UK

Corporate Social Responsibility: From Words to Actions

✉ The Royal Institute of International Affairs, Chatham House, 10 St James's Square, London SW1Y 4LE, UK
☎ +44 20 7957 5754/00   🖶 +44 20 7321 2045/7957 5710   💻 gwright@riia.org
🌐 www.theworldtoday.org/Conferences/cona.html

15–18 October 2001   Wilton Park, Sussex, UK

Improving Accountability and Transparency in Europe: How can this be achieved?

👤 Lorraine Jones, Marketing Executive   💻 lorraine.jones@wiltonpark.org   ☎ + 44 1903 817772

18–19 October 2001   Rotterdam, Netherlands

Triple Bottom Line Investing 2001

👤 Robert Rubinstein   💻 robertr@brooklynb.net   🌐 www.tbli.org

---

23–24 October 2001   Amsterdam, Netherlands

SAI Third Annual Strategic Conference

🌐 www.sa-intl.org

24–26 October 2001   Chicago, IL, USA

8th Annual International Conference Promoting Business Ethics

👤 Dr H. Peter Steeves   ☎ +1 773 362 8770   💻 psteeves@wppost.depaul.edu
👤 Dr John T. Ahern Jr   ☎ +1 312 362 6624   💻 jahern@wppost.depaul.edu
✉ Institute for Business and Professional Ethics, DePaul University, 1 East Jackson Blvd, Suite 6000, Chicago, IL 60604, USA

25–28 October 2001   DePoort, Netherlands

The Role of Business in Enhancing the Prosperity of Humankind

✉ DePoort Conference Center, Biesseltsebaan 34, 6561 KC Groesbeek, Netherlands

✆ +31 2439 71745   💻 register@depoort.org

5–7 November 2001   Berlin, Germany

6th International Business Forum:
Investment, Environment and Corporate Social Responsibility

👤 Erwin Riedman   ✆ +49 (0)30 254 82 127   +49 (0)30 254 82 103   🌐 www.cdg.de

---

7–9 November 2001   Seattle, WA, USA

Business for Social Responsibility Annual Conference:
Learning for the Future

✉ Business for Social Responsibility, 609 Mission Street, 2nd Floor, San Francisco, CA 94105-3506, USA

✆ +1 415 537 0888   +1 415 537 0889   🌐 www.bsr.org

---

23 November 2001   London, UK

Legal Dimensions of Corporate Responsibility

✉ The Royal Institute of International Affairs, Chatham House, 10 St James's Square, London SW1Y 4LE, UK

✆ +44 20 7957 5754/00   +44 20 7321 2045/7957 5710   💻 gwright@riia.org

🌐 www.theworldtoday.org/Conferences/cona.html

27–28 November 2001   Brussels, Belgium

Corporate Social Responsibility (CSR)
on the European Social Policy Agenda

✉ AlteR&I (research and innovation), Rue Froissart 85, B-1040 Brussels, Belgium

✆ +32 2 230 74 28   +32 2 231 15 59   💻 csr@alter.be

5–6 December 2001   Washington, DC, USA

Sustainability as a Business Driver

👤 Oretta Tarkhani, Conference Manager   ✉ World Resources Institute, 10 G Street NE, Suite #800, Washington, DC 2002, USA   ✆ +1 202 729 7750   +1 202 729 7707   💻 oretta@wri.org

---

24–25 April 2002   Johannesburg, South Africa

First Annual African Corporate Citizenship Convention

👤 Sudley Adams   ✆ +27 (0)11 804 1485   +27 (0)11 804 3512   💻 convention@aiccafrica.com

🌐 www.corporatecitizenship-africa.com

7–9 June 2002   Pittsburgh, PA, USA

Conference on International Corporate Responsibility

Catherine Burstein   ✉ Carnegie Bosch Institute, Graduate School of Industrial Administration, Carnegie Mellon University, Pittsburgh, PA 15213, USA   💻 cb6d@andrew.cmu.edu

---

 23–26 June 2002   Göteborg, Sweden

10th International Conference of the Greening of Industry Network. Corporate Social Responsibility: Governance for Sustainability

⊕ www.gin2002.miljo.chalmers.se

Notes for Contributors

THE JOURNAL OF CORPORATE CITIZENSHIP is a multidisciplinary publication and welcomes contributions from researchers an practitioners involved in public policy, organisational behaviour, economic history, strategic management, citizenship, huma rights, corporate governance, sustainability management, responsible supply chain management, stakeholder management, pover gender and globalisation. The journal will reach a wide audience in business, consultancy, government, NGOs and academia

SUBMISSIONS

Submissions via e-mail are preferred if saved as Microsoft Word or RTF documents. These should be sent to veronica.towler(new-academy.ac.uk. Alternatively, two copies and a $3^1/_2$" Macintosh- or PC-compatible disk should be sent to Veronica Towle *The Journal of Corporate Citizenship*, New Academy of Business, 17–19 Clare Street, Bristol BS1 1XA, UK; Tel: +44 (0)117 925 200(Fax: +44 (0)117 925 2007. Hard copies of all figures and tables will be required if the paper is accepted.

PRESENTATION

Articles should be 4,000–6,000 words long. Manuscripts should be arranged in the following order of presentation.

First page:	Title, subtitle (if any), author's name, affiliation, full postal address and telephone, fax and e-mail. Respectiv affiliations and addresses of co-authors should be clearly indicated. Please also include approximately 50 wor of biographical information on all authors, and a good-quality photograph (print, not transparency; black an white preferred; digital files acceptable if at least 300 dpi × 4 cm) of each.
Second page:	A self-contained abstract of up to 200 words summarising the paper and its conclusions; and between 7 an 10 keywords, which will reflect the core themes of the paper (anticipating possible search terms that migl be used by a potential reader).
Subsequent pages:	Main body of text; footnotes; list of references; appendices; tables; illustrations.

Authors are urged to write as concisely as possible, but not at the expense of clarity. The main title of the article should l kept short, up to 40 characters including spaces, but may be accompanied by a subtitle if further clarification is desired. Descriptiv or explanatory passages, intrinsically necessary but which tend to break the flow of the main text, should be expressed as footnot(or appendices.

REFERENCES

All bibliographic references must be complete, comprising: authors and initials, full title and subtitle, place of publication, publishe date, and page references. References to journal articles must include the volume and number of the journal and page exten The layout should adhere to the following convention:

> Clifton, R., and N. Buss (1992) 'Greener Communications', in M. Charter (ed.), *Greener Marketing: A Responsible Approach to Business* (Sheffield, UK: Greenleaf Publishing): 241-53.
>
> Porter, M.E., and C. van der Linde (1995) 'Green and Competitive: Ending the Stalemate', *Harvard Business Review* 73.5 (September/October 1995): 120-33.
>
> WCED (World Commission on Environment and Development) (1987) *Our Common Future* ('The Brundtland Report'; Oxford, UK: Oxford University Press).

These should be listed, alphabetically by author surname, at the end of the article. When citing, please use the 'author–dat method in parentheses, e.g. '(Ditz *et al.* 1995: 107)'.

FOOTNOTES

These should be numbered consecutively in Arabic numerals and placed before the list of bibliographic references. They shoul be indicated in the text by use of parentheses, e.g. '(see Note 1)'. Automatic numbering in word-processing software is acceptabl only in the case of Microsoft Word.

TABLES, GRAPHS, ETC.

All tables, graphs, diagrams and other drawings should be clearly referred to and numbered consecutively in Arabic numeral Their position should be indicated in the text. All figures must have captions. In all figures taken or adapted from other source a brief note to that effect is obligatory, below the caption.

PHOTOGRAPHS

Photographic material relevant to the article is encouraged and should be supplied as prints (black and white or colour).

COPYRIGHT

Before publication, authors are requested to assign copyright to Greenleaf Publishing. This allows Greenleaf Publishing to sanctio reprints and photocopies and to authorise the reprint of complete issues or volumes according to demand. Authors' tradition(rights will not be jeopardised by assigning copyright in this manner, as they will retain the right to re-use.

PROOFS

Authors are responsible for ensuring that all manuscripts (whether original or revised) are accurately typed before final submissio One set of proofs will be sent to authors before publication, which must be returned promptly.

▶ Papers already completed that do not conform to the above conventions may be submitted in their existing format.

▶ **To discuss ideas for contributions,** please contact the General Editor: Malcolm McIntosh, New Academy of Business, 17–1 Clare Street, Bristol BS1 1XA, UK; e-mail: MalcomMcIntosh@btinternet.com.